P9-CQY-393

PLACE THAT PLANT

PLACE THAT PLANT

FRANCES WELLAND

This edition first published in 1998 by
Parragon
Queen Street House
4-5 Queen Street
Bath BA1 1HE

Conceived, edited, illustrated
and produced by Robert Ditchfield Publishers

Text copyright © Parragon 1998
Photographs copyright © Robert Ditchfield Ltd 1998
This edition copyright © Parragon 1998

Reprinted in 1999

Some of the introductory passages in this book first appeared in *The Illustrated Garden Planter* produced by Robert Ditchfield Publishers.

This book is sold subject to the condition that it shall not, by way of trade or otherwise, be lent, resold, hired out or otherwise circulated without the publisher's prior consent in any form of binding or cover than that in which it is published and without similar condition being imposed on the subsequent purchaser.

ISBN 0 75252 429 1 (Hardback)
ISBN 0 75252 430 5 (Paperback)

A copy of the British Library Cataloguing in Publication Data is available from the Library.

Typeset by Action Typesetting Ltd, Gloucester
Colour origination by Colour Quest Graphic Services Ltd, London E9
Printed and bound in Singapore

Half Title: This elegant assembly of plants makes a perfect picture. The formal ornament is surrounded by plants of relaxed shape yet it is buttressed behind and on either side by the clipped hedge and twin box pyramids.

Frontispiece: A clever composition in misty colours for autumn. Michaelmas daisies surf forwards at the front of a border. Their flat rayed flowers make a contrast in shape to the poker heads of red persicaria and white cimicifuga in the background.

THE PURPOSE of this book is to act as an illustrated guide to putting the right plants in the right positions. Its intention is to simplify that most difficult part of garden-making which consists of choosing appropriate plants and planning their combinations.

Ranges of plants are presented in groups according to their attributes and their suitability for a particular setting or soil. Some interrelation is inevitable, and certain key plants may crop up in two or even three sections, as there are many subjects that can be put to multiple use: for example, to embossing a paved terrace or, alternatively, to forming a carpet at the foot of a hedge.

Nearly 800 plants have been illustrated here. The choice is based on many factors. Floral beauty, perfume, grace of leaf, trunk and habit, distinction, suitability for a particular purpose, ease of temperament, all these factors play their part singly or in combination.

Information Given in This Book

Where appropriate, approximate measurements of a plant's height have been given, and also the spread where this is significant, in both metric and imperial measures. The height is the first measurement, as for example 1.2m × 60cm/ 4 × 2ft. However, both height and spread vary so greatly from garden to garden since they depend on soil, climate and position, that these measurements are offered as guides only. This is especially true of trees and shrubs where ultimate growth can be unpredictable.

The following symbols are also used:

E = evergreen
❍ = thrives best or only in full sun
◐ = thrives best or only in part-shade
● = succeeds in full shade
LH = will not tolerate or thrive in a chalky or limy earth and prefers or must have acid, peaty soil to succeed.

Where no sun symbol and no reference to sun or shade is made in the text, it can be assumed that the plant tolerates sun or light shade.

Fully hardy: means that the plant can survive winters in temperate regions.

Not fully hardy: means that it is probable that the plant will need shelter and protection during winter in temperate regions.

Tender: means that even in mild winter areas the plant may need protection to survive or can be grown under glass.

Plant Names

For ease of reference this book gives the botanical name under which a plant is most widely listed for the gardener. These names are sometimes changed and in such cases the new name has been included. Common names are given wherever they are in frequent use.

Poisonous Plants

In recent years, concern has been voiced about poisonous plants or plants which can cause allergic reactions if touched. The fact is that many plants are poisonous, some in a particular part, others in all their parts. For the sake of safety, it is always, without exception, essential to assume that no part of a plant should be eaten unless it is known, without any doubt whatsoever, that the plant or its part is edible and that it cannot provoke an allergic reaction in the individual person who samples it. It must also be remembered that some plants can cause severe dermatitis, blistering or an allergic reaction if touched, in some individuals and not in others. It is the responsibility of the individual to take all the above into account.

Water in the Garden

All water gardens are beautiful, but sadly they can be dangerous, mostly to children who can drown in even a few inches of water, or sometimes to adults. We would urge readers where necessary to take account of this and provide a reliable means of protection if they include water in the garden.

Contents

HOW TO PLACE PLANTS 8

PLANTS FOR SPECIFIC SOILS 14

Plants for Heavy Clay 16
Shrubs and Trees 16–19, Perennials 20–5

Plants for Alkaline Soils 26
Shrubs and Trees 26–9, Perennials and Annuals 30–5

Plants for Lime-free or Acid Soils 36
Shrubs and Trees 36–9, Perennials 40–3

DESIGNING WITH PLANTS 44

Evergreens 46
Prostrate and Short Evergreens 46–7, Large Background Evergreens 48, Conifers 49, Fine-flowered Evergreens 50–1

Architectural Plants 52
Short-Medium Plants 52–3, Medium Height Plants 54–5, Tall Plants 56–7, Substantial Shrubs etc 58–9

Gold and Bright Green Plants 60
Perennials 60–1, Plants for Walls 62, Shrubs 63–6, Trees 67

Grey and Silver Plants 68
Perennials 68–9, Small Shrubs 70–1, Taller Shrubs and Trees 72–3

Scented Plants 74
Shrubs with Fragrant Flowers 74–7, Roses and Climbers 78–9, Annuals, Biennials, Perennials and Bulbs 80–3, Scented Leaves 84–5

Foliage Plants 86
Grasses 86–7, Beautiful-leafed Plants 88–9, Purple-leafed Plants 90–1, Variegated-leafed Plants 92–3

Paving Creepers 94
Mats, Mounds and Rosettes 94–5, Paving Plants with Showy Flowers 96–7, Selected Grey and Silver Foliage Plants 98–9

Alpine and Dwarf Plants 100

Ground-cover Plants 104
Low-growing Plants 104, Short to Medium Perennials 105, Shrubs 106–9

Plants for Difficult Spots 110
Moist Shade 110–11, Dry Shade 112–13, Full Sun and Drought 114–15, Rubbly, Gritty Soil 116–17

A white haze of *Crambe cordifolia* hangs over purple geranium and *Stachys macrantha* 'Robusta'.

THE FOUR SEASONS 118

Shrubs for Seasonal Display 120
Spring 120–1, Summer 122–3, Summer-Autumn 124, Autumn Leaf Colour 125, Autumn Berries or Fruit 126–7

Bulbs, Corms etc Through the Year 128
Spring 128–31, Summer, 132–3, Late Summer to Autumn 134, Autumn, Winter, Early Spring 135

Winter Flowers 136
Shrubs 138–9

Brilliant blue and gold from a partnership of delphinium and *Gentiana lutea* backed by a Japanese maple (*Acer shirasawanum* 'Aureum').

Long-season Flowers 140
Low-growing Perennials 140–3, Perennials up to 1m/3ft 144–5, Shrubs 146–7, Climbers 148–9

Temporary Effects: Annuals, Pots etc 150
Rapid Climbers or Trailers 150–1, Plants Suited to Pots or Tubs 152, Special Trailing Plants for Hanging Baskets 153, Long-season Annuals and Biennials 154–5, Easy Hardy Annuals 156–7

PLANTING A BORDER 158
Labour-saving Perennials 160
Border Perennials 166
Tender Perennials for Sheltered Positions 170
Edge-breakers 172
Perennials for Sun 172–3, Shade-tolerant Perennials 174–5, Shrubs for Sun 176, Shrubs for Shade 177
Back-of-border Shrubs 178
Shrubs that need Wall Protection 178–9, Hardy Shrubs 180–1
Perennials for Pool Borders or Moist Sites 182
Ornamental Herbs 188

TREES, HEDGES AND BACKGROUNDS 192
Hedges: Preparation, Planting and Aftercare 194
Evergreen Hedges 196
Formally Clipped Deciduous Hedges 200
Flowering Hedges 201
Hedging Shrubs for Seaside 204
Low-dividers 206
Hedges for Borders 208
Pleached Alleys 209
Topiary 210
Plants for the Foot of Hedges 212
Bulbs 212–13, Perennials and Low Shrubs 214–19
Screens 220
Bamboos 220, Useful Screening Shubs 220, Evergreen Windbreak Trees 221, Deciduous Windbreak Trees 221
Climbers 222
Evergreens 222–3, Large-flowered Clematis 224, Species Clematis 225–6, Roses 227, Climbers for a Warm Position 228–30, Climbers that Tolerate Shade 231
Pergolas and Arbours 232
Climbers and Their Hosts 234
Trees 236
Trees for Spring Effect 236–9, Flowering Trees for Other Seasons 240–1, Trees with Special Features 242–3, Trees for Decorative Berries and Fruits 244–5, Slim Conifers and Evergreen Trees 246, Large Spreading Conifers for Specimen Planting 247

Index 248

Acknowledgements 256

HOW TO PLACE PLANTS

The challenge that people face when planning their gardens is where and how to place plants that will achieve the effects they desire. In most cases plants will be assembled in beds or borders and the scope for planning these is almost limitless. In theory they can be any shape or size, irregular or formal, anchored to a wall or forming islands. They can be made on the level, sunken or raised. They can be designed as specialist growing areas with imported soil – peat beds, for example, containing lime-intolerant plants in an alkaline garden. They might not look like beds at all but bear a camouflaging top layer of gravel or chippings.

As for the plants, the permutations are even greater. Even in a tiny garden, a mixed border can contain alpines, bulbs, hardy herbaceous plants, tender annuals, biennials, shrubs and, quite possibly, a tree or two. Vegetables and herbs may prove to be necessary additions.

Indeed, the term 'beds and borders' covers so many variables of shape, size and plant life, that it is easy to lose sight of the main common denominator. Beds and borders are collections of plants. To be successful, they must make a collective impact and form pictures.

This is the overriding principle when composing any bed or border, whatever its dimensions and whatever its style. If the border looks as if it is simply a number of individual plants which happen to be growing in the same area of earth, it is a failure.

Other rules of design are rather more flexible and depend on the situation of the beds, on the space at your disposal and, not least, on the amount of time you are able and/or willing to spend on maintenance.

To plan a border, you therefore have to take yourself into account (whether you will weed and water as required) as well as the options your garden offers in terms of soil, space and aspect.

Site

Small beds can be tucked into almost any space providing the soil is suitable, and light, air and moisture are sufficient for good plant growth. Large mixed borders, however, are another matter. The limitations of a garden may be such that only one area is remotely suitable for a border. Nevertheless, if a choice is possible, it helps to bear in mind the following factors. First, that a site open to the sun permits you to grow the greatest range of plants. Second, a big, deep border is far superior to one of ribbon width; 1.8m/6ft is minimum depth for less substantial plants, 3m/10ft more suitable if large shrubs are to be included. Third, a wall, fence, hedge or house-backed border will provide a frame for the picture, an advantage missing in island beds which lack any such anchorage. On the other hand, island sites do give scope for beds which can be viewed from all sides (a point to be taken into account when planning their design). They also have the practical asset of reducing the need for staking, as the stems of plants are less drawn in a bed where light reaches all parts.

Design

It is best to work out the scheme on graph paper first. It will still be hard to visualize this flat plan, so you can either try a sketch or draw the plants onto a photograph of the site.

The airy verticals of verbascum and clary give a relaxed impressionistic effect that belies careful planning.

Foxglove, euphorbia and allium are grouped to form a harmonious colour combination and a wonderful contrast in texture.

However, even this preliminary stage is impossible unless you know your plants. And this means knowing not only the colour of their flowers, but their season of bloom, their foliage, the plants' height, habit of growth and preference for soil and aspect. Given this grasp of the individual, you can then plan the whole.

In the pages that follow, plants are suggested which can be grouped in categories which are useful to consider when assembling a border (such as foliage plants, edge-breakers, winter flowers etc.)

When you plan, you have to visualize not only details like the neighbouring value of two or three plants in terms of their colour and season, but also principles such as how long you want your border to remain in leaf and colour. If it is in permanent view from the house, the answer is probably throughout the year. In this case, refer also to Evergreens on pages 46–51.

The most impressive borders are always designed not just as colour set pieces but to ensure contrast of form and equally of leaf texture. Lacy foliage appears more delicate and refined against plants with entire, leathery leaves. A mass of flowery spires will be stabilized by neighbouring hummocks.

Plant in bold groups for maximum effect.

This formal planting is a splendid example of the powerful effect that can be achieved with a limited variety of plants and a restrained palette.

Generosity of treatment is vital and five of one kind of herbaceous plant in any one spot is not too many, unless the plant is very substantial or the bed unusually small. Such groups, particularly when they have a bold identity and shape, can be repeated at intervals across a border to give a dominant theme in any one season, other plants succeeding in prominence as the season wears on and changing the theme.

Fronts of beds and borders are usually filled with prostrate or low plants, but it is more arresting to allow an occasional tall and clumping plant to infiltrate these ranks. Organized variety is the ideal, not monotonous predictability.

Spacing between groups is rather more a question of experience, but certainly allow some room over and above your spacing of the individual plants. Allow, also, regular spaces for stepping-stones, so that you can enter the bed.

Easy maintenance will depend on the amount of shrubs you can include, and also labour-saving perennials (pages 160–5) which need neither staking nor regular division and lifting. Ground-cover plants (pages 104–9) will be of some use here, too, but with the qualification that their vigour may involve you in having to control their tendency to roam.

Where plants spill over the edge onto

grass and where the setting is suitably formal, it will ease the mower's lot if a line of paving is laid beside the bed, slightly below the level of the lawn.

Tree and Shrub Borders

A border that is composed mainly of trees and large shrubs requires a slightly different approach, for very large subjects are obviously substantial enough not to need grouping. (Smaller shrubs, however, may still require to be planted in masses, if their presence is to be noticed.)

Good design in this kind of border depends greatly on form. Colour is usually a secondary factor. It is always a good plan, however, to include deliberately, some late-flowering shrubs for colour (buddlejas, hebes, eucryphia, hydrangeas, selected roses, caryopteris, perovskia and a further selection on pages 120–7), as most shrubs flower earlier in the season. Autumn colouring or berrying trees and shrubs can also look wonderfully rich at a time when the other inmates are dull or decayed. The ideal is to keep a border in a state of continuous development; fading areas have to be replaced by blossoming, expanding plants, if it is not to become drab, and, being large, dominating the whole garden by its dowdiness.

Terraces and Patios

A terrace or a patio is the sole architectural feature which is essential in most gardens. It has a utilitarian function: to allow the owner to sit, eat and entertain in an area which is adjacent and convenient to the house. Yet, in a large garden, it has an aesthetic and ideal function too, which is to ease the house in stages into the garden beyond, a purpose it fulfils by combining masonry and plants.

Here more than elsewhere, masonry has the upper hand over plants. It is not a place for confusion and plants cannot enjoy the relatively unfettered freedom that may be theirs in wilder or more spacious parts of the garden. Nonetheless they are essential and usually under-used ingredients which will soften and decorate the harsh architectural contours and bring movement and change to the static surface.

It is easier to plan if you visualize it as an area with a clear centre, spacious enough to allow room for your activities or relaxation and for features such as a specimen tree for shade or a small formal pool. Plants can surf forwards luxuriantly over the edges of this area, some rocketing upwards to give vertical contrast to the horizontal lines, others (outside the main traffic lines) encrusting the surface and even encroaching abundantly so long as this does not cause complications. Potted plants can be placed where they cannot grow in the earth and positioned to give a visual balance to other areas.

Remember too that on a drowsy afternoon or at the stillness of dusk, it is the scented flowers that will give you so much pleasure here.

Assessing and Preparing Soil

Soil is either acid, neutral or alkaline, expressed in what is called the pH scale. Its acidity or alkalinity matters because lime-intolerant plants (such as rhododendrons, some heaths, camellias, etc.) will not thrive in an alkaline soil. You can buy soil-testing kits which will assess your soil type.

In other respects, certain soil-types are recognizable by their textures and should be treated accordingly. 1) Sandy soil is light, gritty and dries out quickly. Add peat or compost to improve its ability to hold moisture. 2) Chalky soil is shallow and sometimes has lumps of chalk or limestone in its subsoil. Add compost or rotted manure and

A Japanese maple is positioned against conifers for maximum effect when its foliage reddens in autumn.

fertilizers. 3) Clay soil is heavy and sticky in winter like plasticine, yet dries out in summer to concrete. Dig it over roughly in the autumn to allow frosts to break it down and add strawy compost or organic matter. If the clay is very heavy, it is possible to add garden lime over dry soil. Don't add any fertilizers for at least one month before liming and for three months afterwards. Also, liming means you cannot grow lime-intolerant plants in the soil, nor even in those areas into which the soil or water might leach to any extent.

Planting

The planting season for bare-rooted deciduous trees and shrubs is from late autumn to spring, but if the soil is frozen, very sticky or sodden when the plants arrive, make an earth trench in some spare ground and 'heel in' the plants until conditions improve. Evergreens are better planted in either early autumn or mid-spring when the soil is warmer. Container-grown plants can be planted at any time of the year. Soak the root ball well before removing the polythene and planting. All new plants must be watered regularly during dry spells for up to a year after planting.

Where each tree, shrub or plant will grow, prepare a flat-bottomed hole deeper and wider than the roots will occupy. Put rotted manure or compost right at the base and cover with good topsoil (so that the roots cannot touch the manure). Place the plant in position, pouring damp peat or an equivalent mixed with a little fertilizer around the roots. Don't plant deeper than the soil mark on the stem (with the exception of clematis; see page 222). Firm the soil over the roots when they are covered and re-firm after a heavy frost. Secure planting is always essential.

Trees need a stake placed stoutly in position before the roots are inserted in the hole. Tie the stem to the stake with a soft rubber or cloth tie which will not chafe the bark.

Water all new plants well to settle in, and thereafter keep free of weeds. In dry weather or drying winds, young conifers may need their foliage regularly sprayed as well as their roots watered.

In all cases, a mulch will help to prevent the newly planted subjects from drying out before their roots can establish themselves. But if planting in the depth of winter when the soil is cold, wait until spring before applying the material. Time it so that the soil is still moist but beginning to warm.

Maintenance

A border either has to be under continuous cultivation so that it is kept clean and weed-free, or else you have to find some means of keeping the weeds down if not out. Ground-cover plants, whether shrubby or herbaceous, are one way of doing this. Mulching in spring is another. In this case, allow the soil to lose its winter chill; at that spring stage where it is slightly warmed yet still moist, put on it (around each plant) a thick quilt – from 2.5cm to 7.5cm/1 to 3in deep – of compost, pulverized tree bark, leaf-mould, peat or sawdust. This will also keep the soil moist for longer in the summer, reducing the need for watering. (Mulching is not, of course, used for gravel beds, where the actual chippings serve as a mulch.)

The advantage of leaf-mould, compost, pulverized tree bark and (if you can get it) straw with rotted farmyard manure is that these materials replace nutrients that have been used up by the plants or leached out of the soil. Otherwise, balanced artificial fertilizers can be used.

Staking is also a spring job, though (as a general rule) it is only necessary for plants which grow above 75cm–1m/2½–3ft. In exposed or windy positions, it may prove essential, however, for shorter plants. Brushwood, like pea-sticks, can be put around the plant so that the growing stems will be enclosed and supported by it in an unobtrusive manner. But delphiniums and other tall, very stout-stemmed flowers will have to be tied to stout stakes or canes.

Dead-heading in summer will not only keep a border looking trim, but will prolong the season by inducing the plant to produce further crops of flowers.

In autumn, the woody stems of hardy herbaceous plants should be cut back to the ground. But leave the stems on marginally tender plants, as they may be a small protection in severe winter snaps.

Mauve-blue *Campanula lactiflora* (foreground) and *Salvia sclarea* var. *turkestanica* (background) with sulphur yellow sisyrinchium.

Before the onset of winter (certainly before the likelihood of any hard frost), all tender plants should have a protective covering of loosely packed bracken or grit or peat over the crowns. If they are tall plants, they ought to be wrapped up in a polythene or hessian blanket (ideally with loosely-packed dry straw within). If slugs are a pest, put grit round the crowns.

Plants for Specific Soils

Most plants are adaptable and will grow happily in a wide range of soils. Others, however, are fussier about the medium in which they are grown and some of these have very strict requirements indeed. If you test your soil, you will know whether it is heavy clay, alkaline or acid. This section of the book shows which plants will thrive in each of these situations.

Plants for Heavy Clay

Heavy clay soils are hard to work because they are waterlogged and sticky in winter, yet dry out in summer to resemble a form of concrete. Their other disadvantage is that they are slow to warm up in spring. However, they are fertile and will grow a wider range of plants if the structure can be lightened by the addition of compost or grit which will help to aerate the earth. Ideally this can be incorporated in the spring when the worst of the wet has drained. It is better to avoid working on the ground earlier in the year, because of the nature of the clay. At this time the heavy soil will become compacted if trodden on when sticky.
The following plants will tolerate heavy clay.

Abelia ❍
All forms of this shrub need fertile soil but it must be well-drained. *A. schumannii* is valuable for its late flowering from summer to autum. Needs shelter as not fully hardy. 1.5m/5ft H and W

Betula albo-sinensis. The white Chinese birch tree is noted for its fine rufous peeling bark, light green leaves and airy habit. 15 × 4.5m/49 × 15ft

Aesculus parviflora ❍
The bottlebrush buckeye produces its candles of flowers from mid to late summer. It is also valuable for its changing leaf colour – from bronze when young, to green, to yellow in autumn. Shrubby growth of 3m/10ft H and W.

Betula ermanii
Another beautiful-barked birch, with a pinkish-cream trunk. Glossy leaves colour well in autumn. 15 × 4.5/49 × 15ft

***Chaenomeles speciosa* 'Nivalis'**
Pretty form of 'japonica' with clusters of milky flowers over a long period in spring. 2.1m/7ft H and W

***Cotinus coggygria* (Smoke bush)** ❍
Bushy shrub noted for its masses of tiny flower stalks giving the effect of plumes of floss in later summer. Leaves turn red and gold in autumn. 5m/16ft H and W

Mahonia aquifolium E
The oregon grape is a tough spreading shrub with clustered yellow flowers in spring followed by bloomy purple-indigo berries. 1 × 1.5m/3 × 5ft

Rubus tricolor E:◐●
Low arching shrub with glossy leaves and red bristly stems, and white flowers in midsummer. Useful for ground-cover. 60cm × 1.8m/2 × 6ft

Salix elaeagnos (syn. *rosmarinifolia*)
The hoary willow with elegant silver-green foliage. It grows fast to 3 × 4m/10 × 13ft, so be sure to allow it sufficient room.

***Euonymus fortunei* 'Silver Queen'** E
Shrub which will also climb slowly against walls, with variegated leaves and insignificant tiny cream flowers in spring. 3 × 1.5m/10 × 5ft

***Salix hastata* 'Wehrhahnii'**
Distinctive shrubby willow with dark purple stems studded with silver catkins in spring before the leaves develop. 1.2m/4ft H and W

***Malus hupehensis* (Hupeh crab)**
Robust tree massed with large scented white flowers in mid to late spring, followed by small yellow crab apples in late summer and autumn. It makes a fine, decorative specimen tree. 7.5 × 6m/25 × 20ft

A SELECTION OF SHRUBS AND TREES THAT TOLERATE HEAVY CLAY

Acer platanoides 'Drummondii'
A. pseudoplatanus 'Brilliantissimum' p.236
Aesculus p.16
Alnus glutinosa p.221
Aralia elata p.92
Aucuba japonica p.196
Berberis p.63
Betula (Birch) (some varieties) p.16
Carpinus betulus p.200
Choisya ternata p.48
Corylus
Cotoneaster p.244
Crataegus (Hawthorn) p.200
Eucalyptus p.88
Fraxinus (Ash)
Hedera (Ivy) in variety
Kerria
Laburnum p.209
Magnolia × soulangeana p.237
Malus (Crab) p.244
Philadelphus p.181
Picea breweriana p.247
Platanus (Plane)
Populus (Poplar)
Potentilla p.146
Prunus (Cherry) in variety
Prunus laurocerasus p.198
Pyracantha p.198
Pyrus (Pear) p.73
Quercus (Oak) p.221
Ribes (Currant)
Rubus (Bramble)
Salix (Willow) in variety
Skimmia p.127
Sorbus p.73
Spiraea p.121
Symphoricarpus
Syringa (Lilac) p.181
Taxus (Yew) p.66
Tilia (Lime)
Viburnum p.77
Vinca p.111
Weigela p.93

***Weigela florida* 'Foliis Purpureis'** ❍
Bronze-purple leafed shrub at its prettiest in late spring/early summer with its pink trumpet flowers. 1 × 1.5m/3 × 5ft

***Prunus* 'Kanzan'**
Familiar Japanese cherry tree with ascending habit in youth, spreading in maturity. Prolific with its blossom in spring. Needs good drainage. 10 × 7.5m/33 × 25ft

***Aconitum napellus* (Monkshood)**
A poisonous plant of stately beauty flowering from mid to late summer. Its tall flower spikes may need staking.
1.2m × 45cm/4 × 1½ft

***Aster novae-belgii* 'Harrison's Blue'** ❍
Like many Michaelmas daisies, it may need spraying against mildew. Autumn-flowering. Well-drained soil required.
1m × 45cm/3 × 1½ft

Aster sedifolius (syn. *acris*)
A very floriferous and easy self-supporting bushy Michaelmas daisy. For well-drained soil. Its starry yellow-centred lavender-blue flowers are produced in autumn when they will make a great show.
75cm × 60cm/2½ × 2ft

Campanula latiloba
Easy, vigorous bellflower with leafy spikes of white, blue or amethyst flowers in summer. It will form dense mats and is suitable for sun or semi-shade. 60cm/2ft H and W

Doronicum cordatum (syn. *pardalianche*) **(Leopard's bane)**
Easy, cheerful spring-flowering perennial which forms a spreading clump. 75 × 60cm/2½ × 2ft

Eupatorium purpureum **(Joe Pye weed)** ◐
Very useful, if aggressive, perennial for its flowering in late summer/early autumn. Its height makes it a strong presence in the garden. 2.1 × 1m/7 × 3ft

Geranium himalayense **'Gravetye'**
One of the many accommodating cranesbills, this plant is summer-flowering and vigorous. Plan to include several clumps when designing a summer bed. 45cm/1½ft H and W

Filipendula rubra
Stunning form of meadowsweet with fluffy flower plates in summer. For moist sites. It is another tall plant, which flowers earlier than *Eupatorium* and is less coarse.

***Lamium maculatum* 'Wootton Pink'** E: ◐
One of the 'dead-nettle' family. A pretty and tolerant groundcover plant with pink flowers over foliage which is striped white. It is best in semi-shade and prefers moist but well-drained soil. 15 × 30cm/6in × 1ft

***Hemerocallis* 'Summer Wine'**
Easy day lily with trumpet flowers produced over a long period in summer, though they are individually fleeting. 60cm/2ft H and W

Hosta undulata* var. *undulata ◐ ●
Variegated-leafed hosta with spikes of rich lilac flowers in summer. All hostas prefer moist soil. 45cm/1½ft H and W

Lysimachia clethroides ◐
Vigorous spreader with crooks of white flowers in late summer. Prefers moist soil. 1m × 60cm/3 × 2ft

Lysimachia punctata
This somewhat coarse summer-flowering perennial colonizes moist soil speedily. As the picture shows, it will make a strong clump which may need controlling. 60cm/2 ft H and W

Petasites japonicus ◐ ●
Bizarre flowers in winter/early spring followed by large umbrella leaves. Very invasive. Only for huge spaces where it can be mown out as necessary. 1m/3ft × indefinite spread

Physalis alkekengi **(Chinese lantern)**
Insignificant white flowers are followed in autumn by fruits covered with orange calyces which give it its common name. Invasive. 45 × 60cm/1½ × 2ft

Polemonium caeruleum **(Jacob's ladder)** ❍
Orange-stamened, blue flower-cups in early summer over ferny foliage. It will self-seed with some enthusiam, but is easily weeded out.
60 × 45cm/2 × 1½ft

***Solidago* (Golden rod)** ❍
Perennial forming a clump with sprays of golden flowerheads in later summer to autumn. Most species are vigorous and will make a bold effect in the summer border. Forms include 'Cloth of Gold' (45×60cm/1½×2ft) and 'Golden Wings' (1.5×1m/5×3ft).

Telekia speciosa (syn. *Buphthalmum speciosum*)
Vigorous summer-flowering perennial with large leaves and bold daisy flowers. For moist soil.
1.2 × 1m/4 × 3ft

***Stachys macrantha* 'Robusta'**
Easy perennial flowering in midsummer over wrinkled leaves. Good groundcover. It is shown here with the creamy, feathery plumes of *Aruncus kneiffii*. 45cm/1½ft H and W

Thalictrum aquilegiifolium
Slim stems support fluffy white or mauve flowerheads in early summer above a mound of elegant foliage.
1m × 45cm/3 × 1½ft

Symphytum caucasicum
Easy, lusty comfrey which is coarse but useful in difficult places. It is particularly well suited to the wilder parts of the garden. 1.2m × 60cm/4 × 2ft

CONSIDER ALSO:

Ajuga p.104
Anemone × hybrida p.144
Alchemilla p.52
Astrantia p.161
Bergenia p.52
Brunnera p.92
Caltha p.182
Camassia p.132
Crocosmia masoniorum
Pachysandra
Polygonatum p.219
Pulmonaria p.137
Rudbeckia p.165
Saponaria p.97
Tellima p.105

Plants for Alkaline Soils

Alkaline soil will grow a huge range of plants, though it will deny you the choice of almost all the ericaceous shrubs and trees, like rhododendrons, and a few other examples. It is usually hot, well-drained, and quick to dry out. Many perennials flourish in just these conditions, though larger plants may well require much more moisture than the soil will naturally retain. Incorporating plenty of humus will help water retention; and if this is done repeatedly, it may eventually also lower the degree of alkalinity.

Buddleja alternifolia ❍
A butterfly bush, noted for its long strands of lilac flowers. It can be pruned into a small weeping 'tree' as shown. 3m/10ft H and W

***Buddleja davidii* 'Dartmoor'** ❍
This butterfly bush distinguishes itself by the presentation of its plumes of flowers in elegant arching groups. 2.11m/7ft H and W

***Caragana arborescens* 'Lorbergii'**
Arching elegant shrub, sometimes called the grass tree because of the massed effect of its narrow leaflets. Yellow pea flowers in early summer. 3 × 2.4m/10 × 8ft

***Deutzia* × *elegantissima* 'Rosealind'**
One of the prettiest shrubs with clusters of soft rose-pink flowers in early summer.
1 × 1.5m/3 × 5ft

***Cercis siliquastrum* (Judas tree)** ❍
A very beautiful tree with heart-shaped blue-green leaves and lilac-pink pea flowers in late spring/early summer. Long, green-purple fruits follow on later in the year. 10m/30ft H and W

***Erysimum* 'Bowles' Mauve'**
E: ❍
Wonderful although short-lived sub-shrubby wallflower with blue-grey foliage and mauve flowers recurrently from spring to autumn. 60 × 75cm/
2 × 2½ft

× *Halimiocistus wintonensis* 'Merrist Wood Cream' E: ❍
A lovely shrub for a prominent position, which flowers profusely in late spring or early summer. Not always fully hardy.
60cm × 1.2m/2 × 4ft

Indigofera heterantha ❍
An arching shrub with fern-like foliage and rich pink pea-flowers for a long period from summer to autumn. May be cut down in hard winters. 1.5m/5ft H and W

***Hibiscus syriacus* 'Blue Bird'** ❍
A shrub that is late into leaf but spectacular in flower from late summer to mid autumn. Humus should be added to the soil. Given this, it will grow too in clay. 2.1m/7ft H and W

***Kolkwitzia amabilis* 'Pink Cloud'** ❍
The beauty bush forms a large arching shrub massed with pink flowers like foxgloves in early summer. It has a peeling bark and leaves that turn reddish in autumn. 3m/10ft H and W

***Morus nigra* (Black mulberry)** ❍
Picturesque in maturity, this spreading round-headed tree has heart-shaped leaves. The edible burgundy-red fruits are borne in late summer. Better placed on a lawn than paving, as they can make a mess when they fall. 12 × 15m/39 × 49ft

Paeonia delavayi ❍
A shrub that has most beautiful grey-green foliage and gold-bossed maroon flowers for a short period in early summer. 1.8m/6ft H and W

***Prunus tenella* 'Firehill'** ❍
Showy flowers cluster along the stems of this small shrub in spring. This dwarf Russian almond is invaluable for its warm, bright colour early in the year. 1 × 1.2m/3 × 4ft

A Selection of other Shrubs and Trees for Alkaline Soil

Acer platanoides forms
Acer pseudoplatanus forms
Amelanchier p.236
Berberis p.90
Catalpa p.67
Ceanothus p.50
Cistus p.51
Cornus p.64
Cotoneaster p.126
Daphne p.75
Fagus (Beech) p.200
Fraxinus excelsior (Ash)
Gleditsia p.67
Hydrangea villosa p.124
Koelreuteria paniculata p.241
Laburnum p.209
Liriodendron
Malus (Crab) p.238
Osmanthus
Paulownia
Philadelphus p.181
Populus (Poplar)
Prunus (Cherry)
Pyrus (Pear)
Quercus cerris
Romneya p.147
Rosmarinus p.115
Taxus (Yew) p.199
Teucrium
Viburnum p.77
Weigela p.93
Yucca p.57

Santolina pinnata* ssp. *neapolitana E: ❍
This cotton lavender makes a rounded shrub with aromatic grey-green foliage and yellow button flowers in summer.
75cm × 1m/2½ × 3ft

Xanthoceras sorbifolium ❍
An elegant, unusual shrub with pinnate leaves and white, red-eyed flowers on spikes in late spring.
3 × 2.1m/10 × 7ft

***Achillea filipendulina*'Gold Plate' (Yarrow)** ❍
Dramatic flat heads of flowers in summer which are excellent for drying and will retain their colour well. 1.2m × 60cm/4 × 2ft

Achillea 'The Beacon'
(syn. 'Fanal') ❍
This form of yarrow is a useful coral-coloured alternative to the yellow cultivars. Summer-flowering. 75cm/2½ft H and W

Alyssum saxatile ❍
A vigorous trailing perennial for a wall or rock garden. There is a pale lemon-yellow form called *A.s.* 'Citrinum'. 5 × 45cm/2in × 1½ft

***Anthericum liliago* (St Bernard's lily)** ❍
Delicate white stars rise on thin stems in early summer over clumps of glaucous, rushy leaves. The flowers are quite short-lived but they make a charming impact against a dark background. 60 × 45cm/2 × 1½ft

***Asphodeline lutea* (Yellow asphodel)**
A rush-leafed perennial with spikes of starry flowers for a long period in late spring to midsummer. Its glaucous leaves and seed-heads make it decorative even after flowering. 1m × 60cm/3 × 2ft

***Asplenium trichomanes* (Maidenhair spleenwort)**
A dwarf black-stemmed fern that is often to be found growing in the crevices of stone steps. 10cm/4in H and W

Aubrieta deltoidea E: ❍
A trailing carpeting perennial that will spill colour for a long period in spring over walls or paving. Keep it compact by cutting back hard after flowering.
5 × 45cm/2in × 1½ft

Campanula garganica
A dwarf perennial with starry flowers successionally from summer to autumn. Ideal for walls or paving.
15 × 45cm/6in × 1½ft

***Campanula glomerata* 'Superba'** ❍
An easy vigorous perennial bellflower that will gently self-seed. Clusters of rich blue flowers in summer over soft green leaves. 60cm/2ft H and W

***Centaurea cyanus* (Annual cornflower)** ❍
Wonderful hardy annual which grows easily in any type of soil. Blue, maroon or pink flowers on 45 × 30cm/ 1½ × 1ft branching stems.

***Dianthus* 'Pike's Pink'** E: ❍
One of the many scented pinks which make cushions for a rock garden or at the front of a bed. 15cm/6in H and W

***Dictamnus albus purpureus* (Burning bush)**
A clump-forming perennial with spikes of pink or white flowers in summer. (The oils in the aromatic leaves can be set alight on hot days.) 75cm/2½ft H and W

***Dracunculus vulgaris* (Dragon arum) ❍**
A spreading tuberous perennial with dramatic spathes around a dark spadix in summer. They emit a foul smell after opening which fades after a couple of days. Not fully hardy. 1m × 45cm/3 × 1½ft

***Echinops ritro* ❍**
A stately perennial with globes of steel-blue heads in summer. 1.2m × 60cm/ 4 × 2ft

***Euphorbia myrsinites* ❍**
Trailing stems bear lime-yellow spring flowers. The fleshy blue-grey leaves make a decorative perennial at all times. Not fully hardy. 7.5 × 30cm/ 3in × 1ft

***Linaria maroccana* 'Fairy Bouquet'** ❍
A diminutive hardy annual which makes a charming summer filler in paving gaps. This dwarf toadflax is very easy from seed and gives a dainty effect. Its colour ranges from blue and violet to pink, red and yellow. 15cm/6in H and W

Galega orientalis ❍
A bushy perennial which withstands hot dry conditions. It has spikes of pea flowers in early summer. 1.2m × 75cm/ 4 × 2½ft

***Gypsophila* 'Rosy Veil'** ❍
Tiny pink flowers in summer on wiry stems give a gauzy effect to this low-growing glaucous-leaved gypsophila. 45cm/ 1½ft H and W

***Iberis* (Candytuft)** ❍
A free-flowering dwarf hardy annual which is easy from seed, tolerates poor soil and will be a pretty gap-filler. 15cm/6in H and W

Linaria purpurea 'Canon Went' ❍
The pink form of the usual purple type sending up thin spikes of tiny flowers in summer. It self-seeds gently. 60 × 30cm/2 × 1ft

***Lychnis coronaria* alba** ❍
A short-lived silver-leafed perennial that self-seeds. This white form is less usual than the magenta *L. c. atrosanguinea*. 60 × 45cm/2 × 1½ft

***Origanum laevigatum* 'Hopley's Variety'** ❍
A decorative marjoram with purple-pink bracts around tiny flowers that last for a long period in late summer. 30 × 45cm/ 1 × 1½ft

Scabiosa caucasica ❍
The old-fashioned scabious produces its long thin stems of lovely large flowers in summer. 60cm/2ft H and W

Verbena bonariensis ❍
An open, tall, branching perennial that gives an airy effect. It has clusters of mauve flowers in late summer. Self-seeding. 1.5m × 45cm/5 × 1½ft

A Selection of Other Perennials (including Bulbs) for Alkaline Soil

Acaena p.98
Acanthus spinosus p.54
Allium in variety
Anemone blanda p.128
Arabis
Campanula (most rock garden varieties) p.140
Campanula persicifolia
Coreopsis p.144
Crocus in variety p.135
Eryngium (some) p.54
Euphorbia polychroma p.60
Geranium p.102
Helenium p.168
Irises (most)
Linum narbonense p.145
Meconopsis cambrica p.217
Muscari
Pennisetum villosum
Pulsatilla vulgaris
Salvia nemorosa
Sidalcea p.165
Veronica rupestris
Viola labradorica p.91

Plants for Lime-free or Acid Soils

Some plants cannot thrive in alkaline soil, which is high in calcium. These calcifuges, which are often called lime-haters, become sickly unless they are planted in acid soil. Most ericaceous plants belong to this category and also some other examples which are slightly less lime-intolerant but still need neutral to acid soil. You can assess the kind of soil you have with a testing-kit that reveals whether it is alkaline, neutral or acid. If you have alkaline soil but want to grow a plant that needs acid or neutral soil, a possible solution is to grow it in a container.

Andromeda polifolia compacta E
The bog rosemary is a lovely small shrub with narrow glaucous leaves and pink flowers in late spring or early summer. For peaty soil. 30cm/1ft H and W

***Calluna vulgaris* 'Silver Knight'** E: ○
Excellent ground cover in full sun. Lings flower midsummer to early autumn. 40cm × 1m/ 1ft 4in × 3ft

***Cassiope* 'Muirhead'** E: ◐
Dwarf heath-like shrub with almost stemless bell flowers in spring on upright stems. 20cm/ 8in H and W

***Embothrium coccineum* (Chilean firebush)** E or semi-E: ◐
Brilliant flowers in late spring, early summer on an erect shrub or small tree. Needs shelter as not fully hardy, though the cultivar called 'Norquinco' is somewhat hardier. All need rich, moist soil. 6 × 3m/20 × 10ft

***Erica vagans* 'Lyonesse'** E: ❍
This heather flowers in midsummer/autumn. It is very intolerant of drought. 75cm/2½ft H and W

***Hamamelis* × *intermedia* 'Jelena'**
All witch hazels need lime-free soil. This is a distinctive form with clusters of coppery-red flowers. Good autumn leaf colour. 2.2 × 1.8m/7 × 6ft

***Kalmia angustifolia rubra* (Sheep laurel)** E: ❍
Deep rose flowers over a long period in summer on a slowly spreading bush. 75cm × 1m/2½ × 3ft

***Kalmia latifolia* 'Nimuck Red Bud'** E
The calico bush, or mountain laurel, produces beautiful spring flowers a few years after planting. Full sun for maximum flowering (although it will grow well in part shade), moist rich soil. 3m/10ft H and W

***Nyssa sylvatica* (Tupelo)** ❍
Attractive slow-growing tree of pyramid form with spectacular red and yellow autumn foliage. For sun and moist soil. Resents disturbance, so plant the tree when it is young. 16 × 12m/52 × 39ft

***Pieris floribunda* 'Forest Flame'** E: ◐ ●
The red new foliage in spring (later turning pink, cream, finally green) needs protection from late frosts. 4 × 1.8m/13 × 6ft

***Sciadopitys verticillata* (Umbrella pine)** E: ❍
Distinctive slow-growing conifer, conical in form, with whorls of leaves like umbrella spokes. For soil which does not dry out. 12 × 4.5m/39 × 15ft

***Pieris japonica* 'Mountain Fire'** E:◐ ●
A neat compact form of this shrub with sprays of creamy bell flowers and stunning red shoots which hold their colour well. 1.5m/5ft H and W

***Rhododendron* 'Lem's Cameo'** E:◐
The flowers, pink in bud, appear mid-spring. Needs extra care and shelter lest the flowers are frosted. 1.8m/6ft H and W

OTHER SHRUBS AND TREES WHICH REQUIRE LIME-FREE SOIL

Callistemon citrinus 'Splendens'
Camellia p.50
Cornus canadensis p.104
Corylopsis pauciflora p.138
Enkianthus campanulatus p.125
Pernettya (Gaultheria) mucronata p.109
Fothergilla major p.125
Halesia carolina
H. monticola p.241
Hamamelis × intermedia 'Pallida' p.139
H. mollis
Leucothoe fontanesiana p.93
Lithodora diffusa p.109
Magnolia salicifolia p.237
M. × soulangeana p.237
Pinus radiata p.247
Rhododendron luteum p.77
Rhododendron (including azaleas) p.51

Tropaeolum speciosum ◐
A herbaceous twining climber with dazzling flowers in summer to autumn followed by bright blue fruits. Often grown over a dark-leafed host like yew. The roots must be shaded. 3m/10ft

***Adiantum pedatum* (Northern maidenhair fern)** Semi E: ◐
Delicate fronds spray out on blackish stems. Slowly spreading rootstock. For moist soil and shelter as not fully hardy. 45cm/18in H and W

Adiantum venustum ◐
This exquisite maidenhair fern has pale green fronds. Not fully hardy so give it a sheltered position. For moist soil. 23 × 30cm/9 × 12in

Iris innominata E or semi-E
This beautiful beardless Pacific Coast iris produces its flowers in late spring to early summer. These come in a large variety of subtle colours: pink, blue, purple, cream, yellow, gold. 25cm/10in × indefinite spread

Gentiana sino-ornata E: ❍
Rich blue trumpet flowers on a prostrate autumn-flowering gentian that thrives in moist soil. 5 × 30cm/2 × 12in

Lewisia cotyledon hybrid E: ❍ ◐
Pink or purple flowers in early summer over rosettes of leaves. Winter wet can rot the crown. Protect or plant vertically in a rock crevice to prevent rain collecting in the centre. 30 × 15cm/1ft × 6in

Lilium pardalinum
The leopard lily flowers in summer with nodding turkscap blooms. A vigorous bulb for moist soil which may grow up to 2.1m/7ft.

***Phlox adsurgens* 'Wagon Wheel'** E: ◐
Showy wheel-like flowers in summer on a mat-forming plant that likes peaty, gritty soil.
8 × 30cm/4 × 12in

***Phlox stolonifera* 'Ariane'**
E: ◐
Creeping perennial with milk white flowers in early summer over pale green leaves. Cut back after flowering. 30cm/1ft
H and W

***Pleione formosana* ◐**
Tender bulb but in mild regions can be grown if protected in a very sheltered spot. Flowers on short stems just before the leaves grow in spring. 10cm/4in

***Rhodohypoxis baurii* ○**
Tubers producing pink, red or white flowers in summer. Only frost hardy if kept dry during its winter dormancy but enjoys moisture during its period of growth. 10 × 5cm/4 × 2in

Tricyrtis formosana
An autumn-flowering perennial with spreading rhizomes. Best in humus-rich soil that does not dry out. 60 × 45cm/2 × 1½ft

Trillium grandiflorum ●
The wake-robin forms a clump and flowers in spring. 40 × 30cm/ 1ft 4in × 1ft

Trillium grandiflorum roseum ●
The ravishing pink form of the wake-robin also needs moist but well-drained soil. Trilliums are also sometimes called the trinity flower. 40 × 30cm/ 1ft 4in × 1ft

Trillium sessile rubrum ●
Mahogany-red flowers in spring above mottled bronze-green foliage. Give this lovely variety the same growing conditions as the other wake-robins. 40 × 30cm/1ft 4in × 1ft

OTHER PERENNIALS FOR LIME-FREE SOIL

Blechnum tabulare p.88
Erythronium p.129
Kirengeshoma palmata p.169
Lilium speciosum rubrum
Meconopsis betonicifolia p.169
Meconopsis × sheldonii
Smilacina racemosa p.111

Designing with Plants

When you design a garden, it is your choice of plants that will help give it form, colour, scent and ease of maintenance. For example, beautiful foliage plants will provide interest when the flowers die away and evergreens will give it a winter structure. Scented plants will entice you into the garden and groundcover subjects will reduce your weeding.

Evergreens

It is a cardinal rule that evergreens should form the backbone of a garden, and this is especially true in the area near the house. These are the plants that will keep the garden looking clothed in winter in a northern climate and if they are neglected here, particularly, you will be looking out at a bare area of masonry for half the year.

The best possible use of evergreens is to place them with a view to their collective appearance when all else has withered around them in winter. Don't bunch them all together but space them out around the boundaries, in the corners, near the house and at the furthest point from the house. In this way, you can ensure that the garden looks dressed even in the bleakest months. Vary the type of evergreens, too; choose small as well as tall subjects, conifers but also broad-leafed shrubs, and both delicate and bold-foliaged plants. Supplement the list with evergreen climbers (pages 220–229), with evergreens from gold and bright green plants (pages 60–67) and those plants which have been marked with an E throughout the book.

Dryas octopetala **(Mountain avens)** E: ❍
Mat-forming shrub with oak-like leaves, shining green above, and white, yellow-centred flowers in early summer. 10 × 37cm/ 4in × 1ft 3in

× ***Fatshedera lizei*** E
Shade-tolerant, glossy-leaved plant which is a cross between *Fatsia japonica* and ivy. Lax-growing stems make spreading, prostrate ground-cover or they can be tied to supports to form a shrub up to 2.1m/7ft.

Iberis sempervirens E: ❍
Vigorous, spreading dark green mats covered with milk-white flowers in spring. 'Snowflake' is a good form of this popular sub-shrub. 15 × 60cm/6in × 2ft

Lonicera pileata E: ◐ ●
A small ground-cover shrub with glossy box-like leaves and small creamy flowers in late spring, followed by purple berries. 60cm × 1.8m/2 × 6ft

Mossy saxifrage E: ◐
Pretty, accommodating, enthusiastic carpeters for semi-shade where they will prefer moist soil but endure dry; 'Triumph' has blood-red flowers in late spring. 'Gaiety' is rose pink; 'Pearly King' is white.
15 × 45cm+/6 in × 1½ft+

Azara lanceolata E
A wall shrub or small tree with fanning branches of minute dark green leaves. It bears small, yellow, scented flowers in late spring. It is not fully hardy. 5m/16ft H and W

Choisya ternata E
A shrub with shining, dark green leaves and fragrant, small white flowers in clusters in late spring and sometimes autumn too. Sun or shade. Give wall shelter in very cold or draughty areas. Spreading growth. 2.1 × 3m/7 × 10ft

Prunus laurocerasus **(Laurel)** E
Shade-tolerant shrub with white flowers in spring and glossy green leaves. Will reach 6m/20ft if free-growing but can be clipped hard to form a screen. Its most distinctive form is 'Otto Luyken', which has a low domed habit and narrow leaves.

Lonicera nitida E
Tiny darkest green leaves on a shrub much used for hedging, though it needs cutting up to four times a year as a hedge. Grow at 30cm/1ft intervals to form a barrier. The yellow-leafed cultivar 'Baggesen's Gold' makes an excellent specimen in part-shade. 4m/13ft H and W

***Juniperus* 'Pfitzeriana Aurea'** E
Wide-spreading shrub with strong, ascending branches and gold-green foliage. Very popular and much used to give pronounced, horizontal effects to a design; also useful for its ground-covering, weed-smothering capacity. There is a grey-green form ('Pftizeriana Glauca'), and a smaller form ('Compacta') for those who do not have room for the type plant. 1.8 × 4m/6 × 13ft

Abies koreana E
Compact fir with leaves which are dark green above and white beneath. 6cm/2½in violet-deep blue cones are freely produced even on young trees. 9 × 4.5m/30 × 15ft

***Pinus mugo* (Mountain Pine)** E: ○
Stiff, deep green needles and very small cones on a dense, bushy shrub with spreading habit. Good on poor, limy soils. Slow-growing to 3 × 5m/ 10 × 16ft.

CONSIDER ALSO: conifers on pages 240–1.

Taxus baccata E
The yew is an immensely adaptable tree, used greatly for hedges, for topiary or as a specimen. A free-growing yew would be too large and funereal for a garden, but in a formal setting, several clipped into a neat shape could be suitable. Sun or shade. Size according to pruning.

***Tsuga canadensis* 'Pendula'** E: ◐ ●
Bizarre in growth, this is the low, mounded, weeping form of the eastern hemlock. It tolerates alkaline soil, but prefers moist but well-drained neutral to acid soil. Very slow to 1.8–2.4m/6–8ft or more.

Camellia E: LH: ◐
These are a first choice for soil which is neutral to acid. There are two main hardy varieties, *C. japonica* and *C.* × *williamsii*; the former retains dead flowers, the latter drops them. 'Leonard Messel' (above) is a beautiful hybrid of the *C.* × *williamsii* group, a vigorous, erectly-branched bush, with the glossy leaves common to all camellias. Its flowers are pink with deeper veins, produced in spring. 4 × 3m/13 × 10ft

Ceanothus E: ❍ in variety.
An invaluable (mainly evergreen) group. 'Delight' has rich blue, scented panicles of flowers in late spring, on an erect, fairly hardy bush. 'Cascade' (shown above) is a more tender cultivar with arching growth. *C. impressus* 'Puget Blue' is amongst the best for warmer areas. Autumn-flowering varieties include the tender 'Burkwoodii' and 'Autumnal Blue', which is one of the hardiest. Full sun and good drainage essential. Wall shelter is important, except in warm areas. 2.5m/8ft H and W

Carpenteria californica E: ❍
Dazzling display of white fragrant flowers in midsummer on a rounded shrub with rich glossy foliage. Needs a sheltered position and rich, moist though well-drained soil. 1.5m/5ft H and W

***Cistus* 'Peggy Sammons'**
E: ❍
A floriferous summer-flowering shrub for light dry soil and full sun. It has grey-green soft foliage and charming pink flowers. It is not fully hardy. 1m/3ft H and W.

Consider also *Cistus* × *cyprius*, *C.* × *pulverulentus* and *C.* × *purpureus*.

Hebe E
A group of New Zealand shrubs the finest of which are unfortunately rather tender. The photograph shows *Hebe* 'Simon Delaux' with dark, glossy leaves and purplish-red flower spikes from late summer to autumn; 1.5 × 1m/5 × 3ft. It is a hybrid of *H. speciosa*, like the following fine cultivars; 'Alicia Amherst' (purple-blue), 'Purple Queen' and the magenta-purple 'La Séduisante'. *H. hulkeana* has very long mauve-blue flower panicles in early summer. Hardier varieties include the bronze-leafed, violet-flowered 'Mrs. Winder', and the bright pink 'Great Orme'. 1–1.5m/3–5ft

Ozothamnus ledifolius E: ❍
A bushy aromatic and stiff-leafed shrub with small white honey-scented flowers, orange in bud, in early summer. Not fully hardy. 1m/3ft H and W

Rhododendrons and azaleas E: LH: ◐
These provide a vast and magnificent variety of flowering evergreens, though only for acid soil. The small cultivars are of most general use but nearly all demand part shade. *R.* 'Elizabeth' with rich red trumpet flowers in spring is shown here; 1 × 1.5m/3 × 5ft.

Architectural Plants

Bold-leafed plants are of great architectural value and provide points of reference in an otherwise fussy background. They have the advantage of standing out against stones underfoot, looming walls and perhaps the back of a house too, against an environment which would dominate nearly all other kinds of plants. For these reasons, it is a good idea to include in a garden those flowers and shrubs which are striking in leaf or habit for a good proportion of the year. Evergreens are the most useful of these, for they have a continuous part to play; but herbaceous plants with a definite outline to their foliage are equally valuable, partly because their presence (and absence) in different seasons changes the appearance of the scene. A garden which contains a high proportion of such plants will look shapely, and not simply a collection of oddments.

Alchemilla mollis
Lime-yellow flower-sprays in summer over a mound of leaves. It is a prodigious seeder so remove the flowering stems before seeds ripen. 45cm/1½ft H and W

Bergenia cordifolia E
Glossy, evergreen leaves and magenta flowers in spring. *B.c.* 'Purpurea' has leaves which turn purple-red in winter. Hybrids include 'Ballawley' (shown here) with rosy-red flowers; and 'Silberlicht' with white flowers. 45cm/1½ft H and W

Ferns ◐
Athyrium filix-femina is a deciduous, light green native fern. *A.f.f. plumosum* is a more feathery cultivar and *A.f.f.* 'Victoriae' has crested ends. 75 × 45cm/2½ × 1½ft *Dryopteris borreri cristata* is a graceful, evergreen fern with crests and a stiff, imposing habit.

Helleborus argutifolius (syn. *corsicus*) E
Deeply-cut dark, evergreen leaves with icy green flowers in spring. Vigorous and tolerant of even dry shade. 60cm/2ft H and W

Hosta sieboldiana ◐
Large, blue-grey leaves and lilac flower spikes in summer on one of the most magnificent perennials, making a stately mound. *H.s.* 'Elegans' has bluer leaves. 90 × 45cm/3 × 1½ft

***Acanthus spinosus* (Bear's breeches)**
Mauve and white hooded flowers in later summer rise above glossy leaves.
120 × 60cm/4 × 2ft

***Crocosmia* 'Lucifer'** ❍
A bulb with arching, red crests in summer above sword-like leaves. 'Citronella' is soft yellow. Soil must not dry out. 60 × 15cm/2ft × 6in

***Eryngium giganteum* (Sea holly)** ❍
Self-sowing biennial with silver-blue thistles, silver bracts and spiny leaves. It makes a good subject for cutting and drying. It is tolerant of dry soil.
1m × 30cm/3 × 1ft

Eryngium agavifolium E
This perennial sea holly has narrow spiny leaves and green flower heads.
1.2m × 45cm/4 × 1½ft

Euphorbia characias ssp. ***wulfenii*** **(Spurge)** E
A bold, shrubby euphorbia which needs a position sheltered from buffeting winds. Dark, bluish-green leaves and lime-yellow bottle-brush heads all spring. 90cm × 1.2m/3 × 4ft

Kniphofia **(Red-hot poker)** hybrids ❍
Most have grassy foliage and the best include 'Little Maid' (shown above) with creamy poker heads late summer to autumn. 60 × 45cm/2 × 1½ft

Kniphofia northiae E
This poker has exotic, glaucous, broad leaves in rosettes and cream and red flower spikes in summer. 1m/3ft H and W

***Cynara cardunculus* (Cardoon)** ❍
A stately silver candelabra whose giant purple thistle-heads in summer can be eaten in soups, its stalks blanched and cooked. 2.1 × 1m/7 × 3ft

***Cynara scolymus* (Globe artichoke)** ❍
A shorter version of the cardoon, whose violet thistle-heads can be eaten before flowering in summer. 1.8m × 75cm/ 6 × 2½ft

***Cordyline australis* (New Zealand cabbage palm)** E
In mild areas, this will develop into a small tree with a bunch of green sword-like leaves crowning each branch and creamy flower panicles in early summer. When juvenile, forms a grassy fountain from a central stem. Tender and it will require protection in winter. Ultimately 8m/26ft where it thrives, otherwise 1.5m/5ft.

Onopordum arabicum ❍
Magnificent silver biennial flowering in summer when it reaches to 1.8m/6ft. *O. acanthium* is taller at 2.5–3m × 60cm/8–10 × 2ft. Both self-sow invasively and have sharp spines on their leaves, so may not be suitable in a garden with children.

Trachycarpus fortunei E
Slow-growing but hardy Chusan palm with fan-shaped leaves. Will give a sub-tropical appearance to its surroundings. Ultimately 11 × 5m/ 36 × 16ft.

Yucca gloriosa E: ❍
Thick, grey, spiky and spine-tipped leaf-mounds topped in hot summer by a 2m/6½ft spire of cream bell-flowers. *Y. recurvifolia* is equally tall, but *Y. filamentosa* with hair-like threads on its leaves and the similar but limp-leafed *Y. flaccida* are smaller.

Fatsia japonica E: ◐
Handsome, glossy dark evergreen leaves on a spreading bush which bears creamy flower-heads in late autumn followed by small black fruits. 2.1 × 2.4m/7 × 8ft

Mahonia japonica E: ◐
Shade-bearing evergreen with spiky, dark leaves and lily-of-the-valley-scented, lemon-yellow flowers which appear in early spring. Best in moist soil. 1.8m × 3m/ 6 × 10ft

Mahonia lomariifolia E
Rather more tender than its relative and therefore better placed in a nook between sunny walls in cold areas. Leggy habit, each stem crowned with dark evergreen leaves and crests of yellow flowers in late autumn or winter. 3m × 1.8m/10 × 6ft

Viburnum rhytidophyllum E
Vigorous evergreen shrub with wrinkled leaves, dark green on top and grey beneath; cream flowers in late spring followed by red berries which turn black. Only for very large areas, as shrubs of both sexes must be grouped to ensure fruit. 3 × 3.5m/10 × 12ft

Phormium tenax **(New Zealand flax)** E: ❍
Clump-forming, sword-leafed evergreen perennial forming a dramatic feature. The type has greyish-green leaves topped by a 3.5m/12ft dark red flower spike in summer. Cultivars with purple leaves, or with variegated leaves ranging from cream to dark bronze are available. Not fully hardy. 1.8 × 1m/6 × 3ft

Viburnum plicatum **'Mariesii'**
Tiers of horizontal branches covered in white lace-cap flowers during early summer. Deciduous though the layers of bare branches are distinctive even in winter. 1.8 × 2.1m/6 × 7ft

Gold and Bright Green Plants

It is in the dark and gloomy garden that a mixture of gold and light, bright green leaves comes into its own: golden evergreens and yellow-flowered or -fruited plants are an invaluable way of adding brightness to a dreary winter scene, and gold and green additions will give the impression of soft sunshine on a dull day at any time of the year.

Take care about the kind of flowers you introduce in this setting. Orange and yellow flowers will reinforce the illumination brilliantly. White blossom will cool the brightness. Blue flowers will always seem fresh against golden foliage; this combination is contrasting yet harmonious in a green setting, for green is a secondary colour formed by these two primaries. But never introduce flowers of mixed strong colours in a golden setting for they will simply make it garish.

***Carex elata* 'Aurea' (Bowles' golden sedge)** E: ❍
The leaves of this showy sedge will be brighter in some sun. It requires moist soil. 60cm/2ft H and W

Euphorbia polychroma
Lime-yellow flower heads all spring over bright green leaves which turn pinker in autumn. This attractive spurge is shown here amongst forget-me-nots. 45cm/1½ft H and W

***Hosta* 'Gold Standard'** ◐
A first class vigorous hosta with gold leaves edged finely with dark green. Forms a good clump and retains its colour well. Lavender flowers in summer. 60cm/2ft H and W

***Milium effusum* 'Aureum'** ◐
Bowles' golden grass has gold leaves, stems and flowers. Pretty with spring flowers. Self-sowing. 45 × 30cm/1½ × 1ft

CONSIDER ALSO:

Hakonechloa macra 'Alba-aurea' p.173
Origanum vulgare 'Aureum'
Thymus 'Doone Valley'

***Melissa officinalis* 'Aurea'** ◐
A lemon balm with gold-variegated, aromatic leaves. Keep clipping to promote new yellow leaves. Useful herb, best in semi-shade. 60 × 45cm/2 × 1½ft

***Valeriana phu* 'Aurea'** ○
A perennial with brilliant golden foliage in early spring which turns to green in summer. Its white flowers which are insignificant appear at the same time. 20 × 30cm/8in × 1ft

***Hedera helix* 'Buttercup' (Ivy)** E: ◐
A beautiful form with soft yellow leaves that need at least part-sun to retain their colour. They will green in full shade. 2.7m/9ft

Other golden or gold and green ivies include *Hedera helix* 'Goldheart' (above), *H.h.* 'Angularis Aurea' and *H. colchica* 'Sulphur Heart'.

***Humulus lupulus* 'Aureus'** ❍
A vigorous, golden-leafed hop which grows and colours best in full sun but needs a moist though well-drained position. It is a herbaceous twiner with yellow-green flower bracts. 4m/13ft

***Lonicera japonica* 'Aureo-reticulata'** Semi-E
Fairly vigorous, semi-evergreen honeysuckle with a network of golden veins on its green leaves. Flowers sparsely midsummer onwards, its blooms varying from white through yellow with a purple stain. 5m/16ft

Acer shirasawanum f. ***aureum*** **(Golden leafed Japanese maple)**
A beautiful shrub which requires some shelter. In hot dry situations its rounded, pale yellow leaves are liable to suffer sun-scorch. 3 × 2.4m/10 × 8ft

Aucuba japonica **'Gold Dust'** E
A valuable statuesque plant, dense and bushy, with red berries that are held on the shrub from autumn until spring. 2.4m/8ft H and W

Berberis thunbergii **'Aurea'**
◐
Dazzling yellow in new growth, this neat shrub fades to yellow-green later. It may scorch in full sun. 75cm/2½ft H and W

***Cornus alba* 'Aurea'**
A handsome dogwood with maroon stems and golden-green leaves. Insignificant white flowers in summer. 3m/10ft H and W

***Choisya ternata* 'Sundance'** E
A brilliant yellow form of the Mexican orange-blossom with scented white flowers in late spring. Not fully hardy and needs a sheltered position. 1.5 × 1.8m/5 × 6ft

***Elaeagnus pungens* 'Dicksonii'** E: ❍
A bushy vigorous shrub with glossy leaves that have large central splashes of gold. 2.4 × 3m/8 × 10ft. *E.* × *ebbingei* 'Gilt Edge' has foliage with a golden margin. Both shrubs have small fragrant flowers in autumn.

***Euonymus fortunei* 'Emerald 'n Gold'** E
Brilliant low and spreading bush, staining pink in winter; valuable ground-cover for sun or shade. Climbs if supported. 60cm × 1m/2 × 3ft

Ilex aquifolium E
There are many gold variegated forms including 'Golden Queen' which has bright golden yellow margins to its spiny leaves. It is male, despite its name, so does not produce fruit. 3m/10ft H and W

***Ligustrum ovalifolium* 'Aureum'** E: ❍
The bright golden privet which is at its best when hard-clipped into a compact shape to prevent gappiness at the base. 1.5m+/5ft+ H and W

***Taxus baccata* 'Aurea'** E
A yew of soft gold which will revert to greener tones if grown in heavy shade. 6 × 5m/20 × 16ft. Other yellow yews include the shorter, spreading 'Semperaurea' and a slow-growing Irish yew, 'Standishii', forming a slim column to about 1.2m/4ft.

CONSIDER ALSO:

Juniperus chinensis 'Aurea' p.246
Juniperus 'Pfitzeriana Aurea' p.49
Lonicera nitida 'Baggesen's Gold' p.48

***Sambucus racemosa* 'Plumosa Aurea'**
This shrub has beautiful foliage with scarlet berries in summer after yellow flower-heads. It grows best in part-shade to avoid scorching. Moist soil is necessary. 3m/10ft H and W

***Catalpa bignonioides* 'Aurea'**
Bright copper leaves when new, turning yellow as they age and then greener later in the season. Not for exposed places. Spreading habit. 8m/26ft H and W

***Gleditsia triacanthos* 'Sunburst'** ❍
Bright yellow ferny leaves, greening later, on spreading branches. Fast-growing but best in sheltered positions. Can be pruned in spring to keep tree smaller and induce a burst of young foliage. 12m/40ft H and W

***Robinia pseudoacacia* 'Frisia'**
Bright gold pinnate leaves all summer, but tinting a warmer apricot in autumn. Fast-growing and not for exposed positions. It is one of the most eye-catching of trees for the garden. 12 × 8m/40 × 26ft

Grey and Silver Plants

Leaves in these shades act as a foil to all other colours, whether rich or pastel, primary or secondary. But a silver area or border has in its own right a shimmering effect, seen at its most brilliant against a sombre background such as a deep green or purple-leafed hedge. Here, it will glow especially at dusk, a time of day when the deeper greens of the garden have melted into the darkness.

Not all silver plants are bone hardy (many have their origins in the Mediterranean region), but they do have a practical advantage. Hailing from these hot, dry parts, most are well adapted to drought, a great boon if watering the garden in summer proves difficult.

Grow most of the plants in sun, but the very few that will tolerate shade will make a dark corner gleam with light.

The foliage of the plants shown below varies between white, silver, grey, grey-green and near blue. The texture of the leaves is also remarkable for its variety; some are lacy, others furry or felted.

***Artemisia absinthium* 'Lambrook Silver'** E: ❍
Bush with delicate silver-blue leaves. Spikes of creamy flowers in summer; remove these to induce fresh foliage. 60 × 45cm/ 2 × 1½ft

***Artemisia ludoviciana* (White sage)** ❍
A clump-forming perennial with silver foliage which is at its most dazzling before the spikes of tiny pale flowers form in summer. 1.2m × 60cm/ 4 × 2ft

***Dicentra* 'Langtrees'**
A robust spreading perennial with finely cut grey-green leaves and sprays of pearly flowers in late spring and early summer. 45cm/1½ft H and W

***Dicentra* 'Stuart Boothman'**
A lovely perennial with filigree steel blue foliage and sprays of pink pendant flowers in spring to early summer. 30 × 45cm/1 × 1½ft

Festuca ovina E
Spreading hummocks of blue-grey grass and sprays of small fawn flowers in early summer. May need dividing every few years. Planted closely it can be clipped or mown like a lawn. 25 × 22cm in flower/10 × 9in

***Hosta* 'Halcyon'** ◐ ●
A compact plant with neat heart-shaped leaves of a gunmetal blue. Lavender flowers are borne on stems in summer. For moist soils. 45cm/1½ft H and W

Stachys byzantina (syn. *S. olympica*) E: ❍
Old cottage favourite with very furry silvery leaves, giving it the common name of lamb's ears. Pink flowers on spiky stems in summer. Self-sowing. 45cm/1½ft in flower (× 30cm/1ft). 'Silver Carpet' is a non-flowering cultivar.

Nepeta* × *faassenii ❍
Catmint is an easy plant, much used for ground-cover and edging, with greeny-grey leaves (often eaten back to the quick by cats) and mauve-blue spikes all summer. 45cm/1½ft H and W

Paeonia mlokosewitschii
Mounds of soft grey-green leaves make this peony of foliage value but, for a brief period in early summer, its soft lemon single flowers with golden stamens give it exceptional beauty. 60cm/2ft H and W

Convolvulus cneorum E: ❍
A shrub with pale pink and white flowers in early summer and brilliant silver lanceolate leaves. Not reliably hardy and needs shelter. 60cm/2ft H and W

CONSIDER ALSO:

Acaena 'Blue Haze p.98
Antennaria dioica 'Rosea' p.98
Anthemis cupaniana p.214
Cardoon p.56
Cerastium tomentosum 'Silver Carpet' p.98
Dianthus arenarius
D. gratianopolitanus p.116
Geranium × *riversleaianum* 'Russell Prichard'
Globe artichoke p.56
Hebe albicans
H. pagei
Helictotrichon sempervirens p.86
Hosta sieboldiana p.53
Juniperus communis 'Hibernica' p.246
J. virginiana 'Skyrocket' p.246
Lamium 'Beacon Silver'
Onopordum acanthium
O. arabicum p.57
Othonna cheirifolia p.99
Romneya coulteri p.147
Rosa glauca p.91
Tanacetum densum subsp. *amani* p.99
Thymus lanuginosus
Verbascum olympicum
Veronica incana
Yucca p.57

Helichrysum angustifolium (syn. *italicum*) E: ❍
This aromatic shrub has narrow leaves and is spindly but worth inclusion for its powerful scent of curry. Gold flower clusters on white stems in summer. 60cm/2ft H and W

***Lavandula angustifolia* 'Hidcote'** E: ❍
A lavender that bears flowers of an intense violet 45cm/1½ft H and W. 'Munstead' lavender has mauve flowers, a compact cultivar to 60cm/2ft. Dutch lavender forms the biggest bush to 1.2m/4ft. White and pink-flowered cultivars are sometimes available. The form with the whitest foliage is called *Lavandula lanata* but good drainage is essential.

***Ruta graveolens* 'Jackman's Blue'** E: ❍
Opalescent blue-grey foliage which is beautiful and filigree but may cause dermatitis in some gardeners, Remove yellow flowers in summer in order to keep the shrub compact. 60cm/2ft H and W

Santolina chamaecyparissus E: ❍
The cotton lavender bears palest grey leaves on the plant which should be kept shrubby and compact by being hard-pruned in spring. Yellow button flowers in summer. 60cm/2ft H and W

Salix helvetica
A small twiggy shrub for moist soil with glossy grey leaves and grey then yellow upright catkins in spring. 60 × 45cm/2 × 1½ft

Brachyglottis *(syn. Senecio)* **'Sunshine'** E: ❍
Lax-growing and very spreading shrub with silver-grey-green leaves and yellow daisy flowers in summer. Good subject for banks because of its tumbling coverage. 1 × 1.2m/3 × 4ft

Buddleja davidii **'Nanho Blue'** ❍
Soft grey-green foliage and lavender spikes of flowers in late summer on a shrub which is not quite as quick-growing or large as other buddlejas. 1.8 × 2.1m/6 × 7ft. *B.* 'Lochinch' has paler grey foliage and *B. crispa* has woolly silvery leaves.

Cytisus battandieri ❍
The immensely vigorous though not fully hardy Moroccan broom with silky silvery trifoliate leaves and large golden flower heads in summer, smelling like ripe pineapples. 4 × 5m/13 × 16ft

Elaeagnus angustifolia **(Oleaster)** ❍
Bushy shrub or small tree with penetratingly fragrant tiny beige flowers in early summer followed by small yellow fruits. 5 × 3.5m/16 × 12ft

Hippophae rhamnoides ❍
Silver-grey linear leaves on a large shrub which makes one of the best supports for clematis. The female produces a mass of orange berries if a male plant is placed nearby. 5m/16ft H and W

Perovskia atriplicifolia ❍
A rather lax-growing shrub with finely cut grey leaves and lavender blue flowers late in the summer. Prune in spring. 1m/3ft H and W

***Rosa* × *alba* 'Celestial'**
Vigorous and healthy summer-blooming old rose forming a tall shrub of grey-green leaves. Exquisite shell-pink roses with the sweetest scent. Will tolerate half shade. 1.8m/6ft H and W

***Sorbus aria* 'Lutescens'**
A whitebeam making a handsome tree with silver leaves in spring, turning grey-green in summer. Clusters of white flowers in late spring to early summer are followed by orange-red fruits in autumn. 10 × 8m/ 33 × 26ft

***Pyrus salicifolia* 'Pendula'**
Unique weeping pear tree with narrow silver leaves and small cream flowers in spring. Grows vigorously to form a mushroom-shaped head. 8 × 6m/ 26 × 20ft

Scented Plants

Fragrance is an unseen dimension to plants, invisible but nonetheless very potent. Some plants are imbued with it so that each part carries the scent, whereas in other plants only the flowers are perfumed. A number emit so pervasive a scent that it can be smelt twenty yards away whilst others release their volatile oils only when rubbed or brushed. It will give you the greatest pleasure if you can grow a few of the sweeter scented plants near the house so that their fragrance becomes a constant companion. Alternatively an ideal way of growing these plants is to put them in an enclosure which will intensify their scent.

Buddleja globosa Semi-E: ❍
Honey scented small orange globes are produced in late spring to early summer. 1.8 × 1.2m/ 6 × 4ft

Choisya 'Aztec Pearl' E: ❍
A more compact pretty relative of the Mexican orange blossom (*C. ternata*) with finely cut leaves. Flowers profusely in late spring. 1.2 × 1m/4 × 3ft

***Daphne* × *burkwoodii* 'Somerset'** Semi-E
All daphnes are heavily scented. This hybrid forms a dome and blooms in late spring. Further flowers are sometimes produced in the autumn. 75cm/2½ft H and W

***Daphne cneorum* 'Eximia'**
E: ❍
Prostrate shrub massed with exquisitely scented starry flowers in late spring. 10 × 60cm/4in × 2ft

Euphorbia mellifera E: ❍
Honey scented inflorescence in early summer on a handsome foliage shrub. Not fully hardy and apt to be cut down in hard winters. 1.2 × 1m/4 × 3ft

Lonicera fragrantissima ❍
Twiggy shrub with creamy waxy flowers in late winter to early spring, followed by red berries. 1.8m/6ft H and W

***Magnolia grandiflora* 'Exmouth'** E: ❍
Best grown against a wall in cold areas. The large waxy flowers, like waterlilies, open in late summer. Handsome leathery foliage. 4m/13ft + on a wall

Magnolia wilsonii ◐
Beautiful fragrant but fleeting saucer flowers in late spring on a shrubby tree. 4 × 2.4m/13 × 8ft

Matthiola fruticulosa alba ❍
The perennial white stock has wonderfully scented flowers in late spring and glistening grey leaves. Short-lived but valuable. 60cm/2ft H and W

***Philadelphus* 'Sybille'** ❍
One of the loveliest small mock oranges. Flowering in summer, it has a spreading habit and purple-flushed blossom. 1.2m/4ft H and W

Poncirus trifoliata ◐
The Japanese bitter orange has sparse sharply spined twigs and sweetly scented flowers in late spring followed by tangerine-like fruits. 1.8m/6ft H and W

Rhododendron luteum (*Azalea pontica*) LH
Rich golden flowers in late spring emit a penetrating honey scent for a distance. Good autumn leaf colouring. Like most rhododendrons it should be grown in acid or lime-free soil. 2.4m/8ft H and W

***Syringa meyeri* 'Palibin'** (*S. velutina* or *S. palibiana*) ❍
Excellent twiggy lilac for the small garden flowering in late spring. The fragrant flowers are borne in dense panicles. 1.2 × 1m/4 × 3ft

***Viburnum* × *bodnantense* 'Dawn'** ❍
Deep rose pink buds open into paler, scented flowers from autumn to early spring. A valuable plant for the winter garden. 1.5 × 1.8m/5 × 6ft

***Rosa* 'Constance Spry'** ❍
A modern rose which is only once-flowering though the display of cabbage-rose blooms is dazzling. Scented of myrrh. May need support and can be grown on a wall. To 1.8m/6ft

***Rosa* 'Fragrant Cloud'** ❍
Large heavily perfumed flowers are freely produced on this vigorous hybrid tea rose. The habit of this shrub is upright and it is well covered with mid-green foliage. 1m/3ft H and W

All Gallica roses (old French roses) are perfumed. This is 'Charles de Mills', wine coloured and sumptuous. Its formation is distinctive, as the bloom has a flat, sliced-off appearance. Once flowering. Best in sun. 1.2m/4ft H and W

***Rosa* 'Penelope'** ❍
One of the best hybrid musk roses whose luscious creamy pink flowers are produced over a very long period. 1.5m/5ft H and W

***Lonicera periclymenum* 'Belgica'**
The scented 'Early Dutch Honeysuckle' flowers in summer. The later form, *L.p.* 'Serotina', is equally fragrant, slightly darker hued. Shade the roots. 5m/16ft

***Wisteria sinensis* 'Caroline'** ❍
One of the best scented forms flowering at an early stage of its life (in late spring) and magnificently. 15m/48ft

OTHER SHRUBS AND CLIMBERS WITH FRAGRANT FLOWERS:

Azara lanceolata p.48
Brugmansia p.151
Buddleja davidii p.180
Carpenteria californica p.50
Ceanothus p.50
Chimonanthus fragrans
Clematis armandii p.222
C. balearica p.138
Cytisus battandieri p.72
Daphne odora 'Aureomarginata' p.138
Elaeagnus angustifolia p.72
Jasminum officinale p.148
Magnolia salicifolia p.237
Mahonia japonica p.58
Osmanthus delavayi
Roses
Viburnum × *juddii* p.121

Convallaria majalis ◐ ●
The lily of the valley, a rhizomatous perennial not always easy to establish but spreading by runners where happy. 8in/20cm × indefinite

Cheiranthus cheiri **(Wallflower)** ❍
Scented, spring-bedding biennial plants in flame, primrose, brown, blood-red, pink, purple or ruby. 15–45 × 15–30cm/6in–1½ft × 6in–1ft

Cosmos atrosanguineus ❍
Velvet flowers from summer to autumn with chocolate scent on a perennial that is not fully hardy. 45cm/1½ft H and W

Dianthus barbatus **(Sweet William)** ❍
Scented flowers for summer of white, pink, scarlet or crimson on this easy biennial. 45–60 × 30cm/ 1½–2ft × 1ft. There is also a dwarf variety which can be grown as an annual.

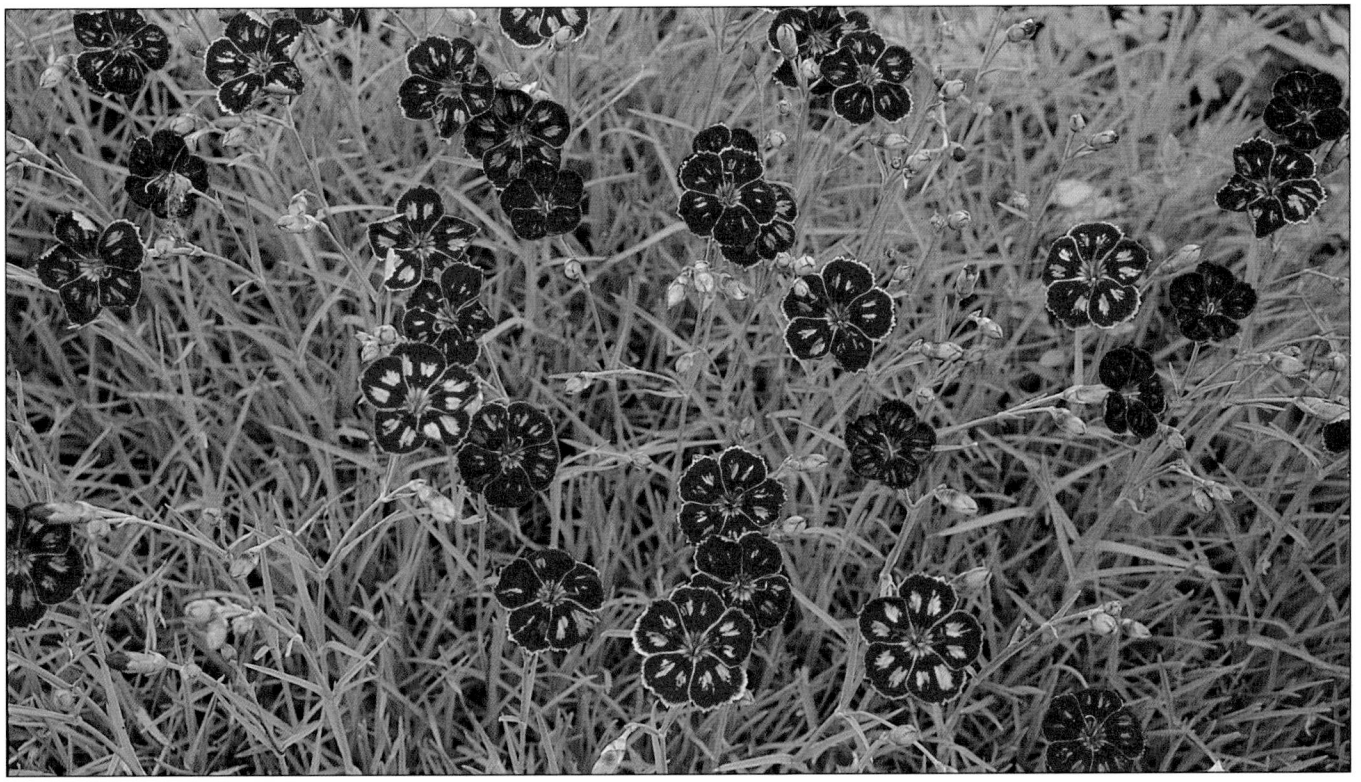

Dianthus **'Gravetye Gem'** E: ❍
Most pinks are scented. This one is clove-sweet and a sound perennial, spreading slowly into a cushion of densely packed blue-grey leaves. Summer-flowering. 15 × 30cm/6 × 12in

OTHER ANNUALS, PERENNIALS AND BULBS WITH SCENTED FLOWERS

Crinum × powellii p.134
Dianthus in variety
Heliotropium peruvianum p.152
Iris germanica p.114
Lathyrus odoratus p.150
Lilies p.133
Narcissus poeticus 'Actaea'
Nicotiana p.155
Phlox paniculata (decussata)
Smilacina racemosa p.111
Viola odorata p.137

Hemerocallis lilio-asphodelus
Day lily flowering in late spring to early summer with sweet-scented trumpets and rushy leaves. 60cm/2ft H and W

Hesperis matronalis
The sweet rocket produces white or mauve heads of blossom in late spring. Self-sows gently. The double form is sought-after but trickier. 75 × 45cm/2½ × 1½ft

***Hyacinthus orientalis* (Hyacinth)**
Stiff and formal bulb in habit but loved for its overpowering fragrance in spring. As shown here, it is a popular subject for formal spring bedding. 20cm/8in

***Lilium* 'Pink Perfection'**
Voluptuously scented trumpet flowers in summer on a bulb that grows to 1.2m/4ft or more. Grow it in a pot so that it can be placed in an appropriate position in the garden. Here it is shown in front of white hydrangeas.

***Matthiola* (Stock) ❍**
There are annual stocks, but the biennial is the Brompton stock, branching plants in shades of white, pink, carmine, mauve or purple with a rich scent. The flowering time is early summer. 45 × 37cm/1½ft × 1ft 3in

***Narcissus tazetta* ❍**
A variable species, blooming from late autumn to mid-spring. The well-known tender 'Paper White', with glistening white very fragrant flowers often forced for winter, is a cultivar. Jonquils, another group of narcissi, are also very scented. Of the double daffodils, 'Sir Winston Churchill' (white with orange florets) is fragrant and a good garden plant.

Chamaemelum nobile ❍
Chamomile, a ground cover plant, is sometimes substituted for grass as a small lawn. The form 'Treneague' does not flower. Best in light soil. 15cm/6in H and W

Mint
A collection of scented plants must include mints. This decorative form is the variegated apple mint, *Mentha suaveolens* 'Variegata'. It has a running rootstock. Best in shade. 60cm/2ft

Pelargonium tomentosum ◐ ●
Emerald velvet leaves smell of peppermint. Cut off the insignificant white flowers to encourage fresh foliage. Sprawling and tender. 1m/3ft

***Pelargonium* 'Mabel Grey'** ❍
One of the most strongly lemon-scented 'geraniums' with rough serrated leaves. Pinch out the flowers to encourage foliage. Tender. 1m/3ft

***Pelargonium* 'Purple Unique'** ❍
A robust tender shrub which can be grown against a wall under glass. The lobed leaves have a musty smell. 1m/3ft+

OTHER PLANTS WITH AROMATIC LEAVES INCLUDE:

Artemisia abrotanum
Eucalyptus p.88
Foeniculum vulgare (Fennel) p.189
Helichrysum angustifolium
Hyssopus officinalis (Hyssop) p.189
Laurus nobilis (Bay) p.210
Lavandula sp. (Lavender) p.207
Melissa officinalis 'Aurea' (Lemon balm) p.61
Monarda (Bergamot)
Origanum vulgare 'Aureum' (Oregano)
Ruta graveolens (Rue) p.71
Salvia officinalis (Sage)
Satureja montana (Winter savory)

Foliage Plants

The most successful gardens are those with a generous proportion of fine foliage plants (regardless whether they flower or not). Flowers are in bloom for only a relatively brief period, but graceful foliage will last for a minimum of six months and will prevent an area decaying into tat late in the season.

Of the groups below, use the grasses as quiet foils which will moderate strong hues in flowers, or plant them to act as a barrier between clashing neighbours. Also position them to make an arresting vertical contrast to plants with horizontally held leaves. Put the beautiful leafed plants beside subjects of coarser appearance to throw their own refinement into relief.

Plant the purple-leafed plants as a strong background contrast to pale companions such as the variegated-leafed plants which are the more curious for having plain neighbours. Or use the purple subjects to intensify a border composed of red flowers.

In addition to the plants on the following pages, it is worth considering the subjects listed in Architectural Plants on pages 52–9.

Helictotrichon sempervirens (syn. *Avena candida*) **(Blue oat grass)** E:O
Neat, vivid blue-grey clumps with arching sprays of 'oats' in early summer. 45 × 30cm/ 1½ft × 1ft (1m/3ft in flower)

Carex comans **(bronze form)**
A stunning low-growing mophead sedge, the colouring of which is at its most intense in winter. Frost only serves to make it more beautiful. 60cm/2ft H and W

***Spartina pectinata* 'Aureomarginata'**
A vigorous striking grass with yellow-striped leaves which appreciates moist soil where its rhizomes will spread indefinitely. Greenish flower-spikes with purple stamens in summer. 1.8m/6ft

***Miscanthus sinensis* 'Silver Feather'**
A very free-flowering form of a clump-forming grass which bears tall pale plumes of flowering spikes in autumn above the fountain of leaves.
1.8 × 1.2m/6 × 4ft

Stipa tenuissima ❍
A shape of fountain-like grace and soft wispy seedheads in summer make this an attractive grass to include in a bed or border. 60 × 45cm/2 × 1½ft

Stipa gigantea E
Evergreen foliage with spraying appearance from which tall feathery buff plumes rise in summer. 75cm × 1m/2½ft × 3ft, and 1.8m/6ft high in flower

***Acer palmatum* 'Dissectum'**
A beautiful Japanese maple with very finely divided leaves, eventually forming an elegant mound. It turns a rich red in autumn. Can scorch in a hot position.
1 × 1.5m/3 × 5ft

Blechnum tabulare E: LH: ◐
This fern makes good running ground cover for moist neutral to acid soil. It is not fully hardy so requires a sheltered position. 60 × 45cm/ 2 × 1½ft

Eucalyptus gunnii E: ❍
An Australian evergreen tree which, if kept pruned as a shrub, will continue to produce its small, round, blue juvenile leaves. Keep to 1.5m/5ft in height if used for foliage.

***Artemisia* 'Powis Castle'**
Semi-E: ❍
Exquisite silver-grey leaves of lacy texture on a cultivar which is the hardiest form of this shrub. Sun, shelter and good drainage are required. 75cm × 1m/ 2½ × 3ft

***Polystichum setiferum* Plumosodivisilobum ◐ ●**
This form of the soft shield fern has perhaps the most glamorous of all leaves as they are softly textured and very finely divided, spraying out to form a low mound. 45 × 60cm/1½ × 2ft

***Sambucus* 'Notcutt's Variety'**
A small shrub which is a filigree-leafed form of elder and an effective and untricky substitute for the cut-leafed *Acer palmatum* 'Dissectum'. 1m/3ft H and W

***Veratrum nigrum* ◐**
Large ribbed green leaves make a stunning and majestic foliage plant with spikes of maroon flowers on tall stems in late summer. (*V. album* has white flowers.) A perennial for moist soil. 1.5m × 60cm/ 5 × 2ft

***Anthriscus sylvestris* 'Ravenswing'**
Like a refined and beautiful cow parsley, this perennial makes an airy fountain of filigree leaves with umbels of white lace flowers in early summer. 1m × 60cm/3 × 2ft

***Acer palmatum* 'Dissectum Atropurpureum'**
Hummocky shrub with very finely cut purple-bronze leaves reddening in the autumn. This is the dark form of the plain green cultivar (*A.p. 'Dissectum'*) shown on page 88. 1 × 1.5m/3 × 5ft

***Berberis thunbergii* 'Rose Glow'**
Prettiest of the purple-leafed berberis with new growth on the shrub speckled with pale and deep pink before darkening. Bushy. 1.2m/4ft H and W

***Cotinus coggygria* 'Royal Purple' (Smoke tree)**
Very dark-foliaged shrub with feathery pink flowers in summer that resemble puffs of smoke. The leaves turn rich red in autumn. 4m/13ft H and W

***Heuchera* 'Palace Purple'**
Beautiful perennial with dark scalloped leaves and cream flower sprays in early summer. 45cm/1½ft H and W

Rosa glauca A shrub rose, and one of the most delicate subjects in this category, with mauve-grey leaves and, in midsummer, small pink, white-centred, single flowers followed by red fruits. 1.8 × 1.2m/ 6 × 4ft

CONSIDER ALSO:

Cordyline australis 'Atropurpurea' p.56
Malus × *moerlandsii* 'Profusion' p.238
Weigela florida 'Foliis Purpureis' p.19

Viola labradorica E
An invaluable spreading and self-seeding little plant (good everywhere except invading a precious rockery) with dark leaves and, in spring and early summer, pale violet scentless flowers. Happy in sun or shade. 15cm/6in H and W

Sedum maximum atropurpureum ❍
Bronze-purple succulent leaves on red stems with a sadly drooping habit. Pale pink flower heads in late summer to autumn. 45 × 30cm/1½ × 1ft

***Aralia elata* 'Variegata'**
Oustanding shrub or small tree with margined-white leaves and foaming sprays of white flowers in late summer. There is also a yellow-variegated form called 'Aureovariegata' of this Japanese angelica tree.
3.5 × 3m/12 × 10ft

***Brunnera macrophylla* 'Variegata'** ◐
Eye-catching cream and green leaves (some almost entirely cream) on a herbaceous plant with blue flowers in spring.
45 × 30cm/1½ × 1ft

***Cornus alba* 'Elegantissima'**
Useful shrub with white marked grey-green leaves. Suitable as a companion for neighbouring dark-leafed shrubs. 3m/10ft H and W

***Leucothöe fontanesiana* 'Rainbow'** E: LH: ◐
Handsome evergreen shrub for acid soils with glossy, purple-green leaves bearing pink, yellow and cream variegation. Drooping sprays of white flowers in late spring. 75cm × 1m/2½ × 3ft

Consider also the selection of variegated shrubs shown in Gold and Bright Green Plants, pages 60–7.

***Symphytum* × *uplandicum* 'Variegatum'**
This variegated comfrey with its dazzling cream-margined green leaves and blue-mauve flowers in high summer catches attention. Cut out any plain green leaves.
75 × 45cm/2½ × 1½ft

***Weigela florida* 'Variegata'** ❍
An exceedingly pretty, bushy shrub the leaves of which have fine cream margins. Soft pink flowers in early summer when it is one of the most attractive plants in the garden. 1.5m/5ft H and W

Paving Creepers

When a garden is laid with paving slabs, bricks, cobbles, gravels or any other type of hard material, it will look bleak unless this unrelieved ground surface is mellowed with small or prostrate plants. They are particularly useful for breaking up the rigid appearance of square or rectangular paving which is so often laid with monotonous regularity. A few of these little plants don't mind being walked on (especially thymes), but for the most part they are best inserted around the main areas of traffic. Their actual planting presents a problem if the masonry has been set in solid cement; in this case, all you can do is force out chunks of the mortar with a crowbar, replace it with earth and then insert the plants most tolerant of poor, arid conditions and keep them fed and watered until they have rooted down. The plants will have to be kept well watered until the roots have made a home for themselves.

Armeria maritima **(Thrift)**
E: ❍
Pin-cushion flowers in summer above vigorous, easy, spreading grassy mounds. There are white, pale pink and brick red forms too. 10 × 30cm/ 4in × 1ft

Androsace lanuginosa E or semi-E: ❍
Beautiful mat-forming perennial with a trailing habit. Small heads of blush or lilac dark- or yellow-eyed flowers for a long period in summer. Happy on gravel. 5 × 30cm/2in × 1ft

***Sagina subulata* 'Aurea'** E: ❍
A spreading mat of golden foliage completely spangled with minute white flowers in summer. For moist gritty soil. 2 × 30cm/1in × 1ft

***Sedum spurium* 'Dragon's Blood'** E: ❍
Forms quick-growing carpets of green rosettes with rich red sprays of flowers in summer. 10 × 50cm/4in × 1 ft 8in. Nearly all sedums are ideal for hot, dry positions in full sun and for enlivening paving, paths, steps and walls.

***Thymus serpyllum* 'Coccineus'** E
Red flowers in summer above a carpet of tiny, scented leaves. Other excellent varieties for paving are 'Doone Valley' with gold-splashed foliage and *T. lanuginosus* with very woolly grey mats sprinkled with lilac-pink flowers in summer. 5 × 30cm+/2in × 1ft+

***Sempervivum arachnoideum* 'Laggeri'** E: ❍
One of the most delicately formed of the houseleeks, with silver cobwebs on its small rosettes and pink flowers in summer. 10 × 15cm/4 × 6in. Sempervivums endure hot, dry conditions and are ideal crevice fillers in sun.

***Trifolium repens* 'Purpurascens' (Purple-leafed clover)** ❍
Vigorous mat-forming purple variety of the common clover which will run between paving. It has white flowers in summer. 5 × 45cm/2in × 1½ft

Campanula cochleariifolia ❍
A charming tiny bellflower with a running habit and massed stems of small blue, or slate or white flowers in summer. 5 × 60cm/2in × 2ft

Dianthus deltoides E: ❍
The maiden pink forms a wide evergreen mat with crimson (or white or coral) flowers in summer. The white or blush-flowered *D. arenarius* with grassy grey leaves and *D. gratianopolitanus* shown on p. 116 are also ideal.
15 × 30cm/6in × 1ft

Campanula poscharskyana E
As vigorous as a weed, which is fine for paving cracks. Blue, starry flowers all summer and autumn in sun or shade above spreading mats. 12 × 60cm/5in × 2ft

***Helianthemum* 'Annabel'** E: ❍
A lovely double form of the rock rose with grey-green leaves. Most varieties are single and the flowers don't last as long. A spreading drought-tolerant plant.
20 × 40cm/8in × 1ft 4in

Parahebe catarractae E: ❍
Enthusiastic sub-shrub massed with mauve, or in another form, white, flower-sprays zoned with purple-red. For a sheltered position as it is not fully hardy.
30 × 45cm/1 × 1½ft

***Phlox subulata* 'Emerald Cushion'** E
Vigorous, mat-forming plant sheeted with flowers in spring. White, pink, crimson, lavender and violet-flowered cultivars are also obtainable. 10cm/4in H and spread varies 20–45cm/8in–1½ft.

Saponaria ocymoides
Semi-E: ❍
Very vigorous, spreading or trailing mat of small green leaves with showers of pink flowers in summer.
15 × 60cm/6in × 2ft

Veronica prostrata (syn. *rupestris*) E
Very vigorous, spreading or trailing mat-forming plant (ideal for steps) with rich blue flower spires in early summer. 10 × 30cm/4in × 1ft

***Acaena* 'Blue Haze'** E
Very spreading, grey-leafed, red-stemmed plant for poor, dry soils. 8cm/3½in. *A. adscendens* is an even more rampant sprawler over paving. 12 × 90cm/5in × 3ft

***Antennaria dioica* 'Rosea'** E : ❍
Another mat-former with fluffy pink flower-heads in early summer and grey-green, silver-edged leaves. 12 × 60cm/5in × 2ft. *A. aprica* (syn. *parvifolia*) bears white flowers.

***Cerastium tomentosum* 'Silver Carpet'** E
Small white flowers on thin stems in summer over grey-leafed mats. Desperately invasive and needs confining or can be used as a last resort where little else will grow or is grown. 15cm/6in × indefinite spread

Tanacetum densum subsp. ***amani*** (syn. *Chrysanthemum haradjanii*) E: ❍
Most beautiful mats of feathery, silver foliage. Small yellow flowers in summer. Not fully hardy.
10 × 45cm/4in × 1½ft

Othonna (syn. *Othonnopsis*) ***cheirifolia*** E: ❍
Fleshy, grey, erectly held leaves on a plant with a trailing habit. Good for sunny steps. Yellow daisy flowers in summer. Not fully hardy. 30cm/1ft H and W

Veronica spicata subsp. ***incana*** Semi-E: ❍
Spikes of sprawling bright blue flowers in summer appear above pointed leaves which are covered in silver hairs. 30cm/1ft H and W

Alpine and Dwarf Plants

Any gardener who wants to grow a large range of plants in a small space might consider specializing in alpines or dwarf plants. Conventionally these were grown in rock gardens, but the odd style of these gardens – the disruptive appearance of a group of rocks in otherwise flat surroundings – has encouraged other ways of growing alpines in recent decades. Raised beds or walls for trailing plants, or sinks and troughs for tiny subjects, or specially prepared peat beds for plants that are lime-intolerant are all attractive possibilities that are probably easier to accommodate in most gardens.

Alyssum spinosum roseum ❍
A little spiny silver-green shrublet with clusters of pink flowers in summer forming a low mound. It is suited to a large trough, as shown. 20 × 30cm/ 8in × 1ft

***Campanula* 'Birch Hybrid'**
A showy vigorous spreader, good hanging over a wall, with open violet-blue bellflowers en masse in summer for a long period and small toothed leaves. 15 × 45cm/ 6in × 1½ft

Crassula sarcocaulis E, ❍
A gnarled shrublet with spiky succulent leaves and starry pink flowers, useful for their late-summer flowering. Not fully hardy but is worth trying in a well-drained sheltered spot. 20cm/8in H and W

Dodecatheon meadia **(Shooting star)** ◐
Rich rose flowers with prominent stamens bloom on thin stems in spring over rosettes of leathery leaves. For moist soil. 25 × 15cm/10 × 6in

Dicentra cucullaria
A real charmer with milky, thickly textured flowers in spring like little butterflies above glaucous ferny leaves. It dies down soon after flowering. 15cm/6in H and W

Erodium guttatum ❍
A small silver leafed perennial or sub-shrub which bears distinctive flowers in summer, blush white with two darkly blotched upper petals. 10 × 20cm/4 × 8in

***Erodium* 'Merstham Pink'** ❍
A very pretty form with pink flowers in summer. Like all erodiums it needs good drainage. 15 × 25cm/6 × 10in

***Geranium cinereum* var. *subcaulescens* 'Splendens'** ❍
A dazzling dwarf with dark-eyed flowers in summer. 10 × 25cm/4 × 10in

Euryops acraeus ❍
A showy bushlet of sparkling silver-green leaves with massed golden daisies in early summer. Not fully hardy. 10 × 20cm/4 × 8in

***Hebe* 'Boughton Dome'** E: ❍
An evergreen shrub with the appearance of a conifer, this hebe is grown for its smoothly rounded formation. Slow growing. 45cm/1½ft H and W, though eventually larger.

Hypericum olympicum ❍
A neat bush with grey-green leaves and golden flowers in early summer. Needs good drainage. 20 × 25cm/8 × 10in

Moltkia suffruticosa ❍
A little sub-shrub with nodding heads of rich blue flowers in early summer and dark green leaves.
25 × 30cm/10in × 1ft

***Picea abies* 'Gregoryana'**
E: O
A tiny domed conifer, small enough to include in a trough or sink. 30cm/1ft H and W

***Sedum spathulifolium* 'Cape Blanco'** E: ❍
A dazzling sedum forming rosettes of silver leaves which are covered with yolk-yellow starry flowers in summer.
7.5 × 20cm/3 × 8in

***Veronica pinnata* 'Blue Eyes'**
Enjoying a leafier soil than most alpines, it sends up spires of small, intensely blue flowers in spring and early summer.
10 × 30cm/4in × 1ft

CONSIDER ALSO:

Androsace lanuginosa p.94
Antennaria dioica 'Rosea' p.98
Aubrieta deltoidea p.31
Campanula garganica p.31
Cassiope 'Muirhead' p.36
Cyclamen coum p.136
Dianthus 'Pike's Pink' p.32
Daphne cneorum 'Eximia' p.15
Euphorbia myrsinites p.33
Gentiana sino-ornata p.40
Lewisia cotyledon p.41
Phlox adsurgens 'Wagon Wheel' p.41
Phlox 'Emerald Cushion' p.97
Rhodohypoxis baurii p.42
Sempervivum p.117
Tanacetum densum subsp. *amani* p.99

Ground-cover Plants

Ground-cover plants, whether shrubs or perennials, are subjects whose habit of dense growth suppresses the weeds which might grow beneath them. If you confine your plantings to weed-suppressors only, you will achieve the kind of garden that is nearly labour-free.

Almost any plant whose skirt comes right down to the ground and is evergreen (or, if herbaceous or deciduous, is nonetheless densely leafy) qualifies as a weed-suppressor. So a large number of other plants mentioned elsewhere in this book will fulfil this role and you can use these to supplement the list below of effective shrubs and perennials. However, in all cases, the ground has to be kept weed-free until the plants establish themselves, join up and take over the job themselves. After this stage your only task will be to curb by cutting back (or digging up) the more vigorous plants which threaten to ramp outside their territory.

***Cornus canadensis* (Creeping dogwood)** LH
Plant for sun or shade but needs peaty, lime-free soil. Creamy-white flower bracts in early summer followed by clustered red berries. 15 × 60cm/ 6in × 2ft

***Dicentra* 'Bacchanal'** ◐ ●
Very accommodating running herbaceous plant with bright green leaves and pendent crimson flowers in spring to summer for a long period. 45cm/1½ft H and W

***Ajuga reptans* 'Pink Surprise'** E
Neat carpeter with bright pink flower spikes in late spring and bronze leaves. 15 × 60cm/6in × 2ft. There are also several other cultivars, the best of which is 'Burgundy Glow'. 10 × 45cm/4in × 1½ft

Epimedium E: ◐ in variety
All excellent for cool, shady positions. *E. youngianum* has white flowers in the form 'Niveum' (shown above), *E. grandiflorum* 'Rose Queen' is pink, both blooming in late spring. Other epimediums bear similarly shaped flowers in yellow, orange, red or mauve. One of the most vigorous is the yellow *E. perralderianum*. 30cm/1ft H and W

Geranium in some variety
G. endressii is one of the best, a colonizer in sun or shade, bearing a perpetual succession of pink flowers. 45 × 60cm/1½ × 2ft. Other good varieties include *G.* 'Johnson's Blue' (shown on p. 162) and *G. macrorrhizum* (shown on p. 174)

CONSIDER ALSO:
Alchemilla mollis p.52
Bergenia p.52
Hellebores in variety
Hosta in variety

***Persicaria bistorta* 'Superba'**
Vigorous and even rampant in moist soil with pink poker flower spikes in summer and sometimes autumn also, over light green leaves. 1m × 60cm/3 × 2ft

***Rodgersia pinnata* 'Superba'** ◐
A most beautiful foliage plant for moist even boggy soils. This has pink fluffy flowers in summer over leaves which resemble those of a horse chestnut. Almost all rodgersias make good ground-cover. 1m/3ft H and W

Tellima grandiflora E: ◐ ●
Clump-forming plant with hairy, scalloped leaves and spires of cream and green bell-flowers in late spring. The form 'Purpurea' has bronze leaves. 60 × 30cm/ 2 × 1ft

Ceratostigma plumbaginoides ❍
A running sub-shrub with a succession of bright blue flowers in autumn when the leaves colour hotly.
15 × 60cm/6in × 2ft

Cotoneaster dammeri E: ◐
A dense ground hugging evergreen mat with red fruits in autumn, following minute white flowers in spring.
30cm × 3m/1ft × 10ft

Cytisus × kewensis ❍
Prostrate and spreading broom which is laden with sprays of creamy-yellow flowers in late spring. Its arching habit makes it suitable for covering a bank.
25cm × 1m/10in × 3ft

Heathers in variety; E: most LH.
The dwarf *Erica* and *Calluna* are amongst the most commonly planted groups for ground cover. *Erica carnea* (shown above) with red, white or pink flowers and green or golden foliage is lime-tolerant. Winter/spring flowers. 30 × 45cm/1 × 1½ft

Erica* × *darleyensis is also lime-tolerant. It flowers in winter to early spring. 45cm × 1m/1½ × 3ft.

Hebe in some variety: E.
H. rakaiensis (syn. *subalpina*) is one of the best for this purpose, forming a small-leafed, evergreen, apple-green hummock with small white flowers in summer. 75cm × 1m/2½ × 3ft

***Juniperus horizontalis* 'Wiltonii' ('Blue rug')** ❍
There are many ground-hugging junipers, all enjoying sun and good drainage. The whipcord foliage of this variety can become tinged with purple in winter.
30cm × 1.8m/1 × 6ft

***Hypericum calycinum* (Rose of Sharon)** E or Semi-E
This is an invasive shrub (occasionally subject to rust) so is best confined to those areas such as slopes where few other plants will cope. 30cm × 1.5m/ 1 × 5ft

Juniperus sabina tamariscifolia E: ❍
Very spreading conifer forming a flat top; foliage is grey when young but a rich green later. 1m × 2m/3 × 6½ft.
See also *J.* 'Pfitzeriana Aurea' on p. 49.

***Lithodora diffusa* 'Heavenly Blue'** E: LH: ❍
A large, small-leafed mat covered with bright blue flowers over a long period from late spring onwards. Needs good drainage and lime-free soil.
7.5cm × 60cm/3in × 2ft

Gaultheria (syn. *Pernettya*) ***mucronata*** E: LH: ◐
Showy evergreen for acid soils, forming dense suckering thickets. Small white heath-like flowers in spring followed by clusters of berries from white to pink or cherry-red. Plant in groups to ensure fruiting. 75cm × 1.2m/ 2½ × 4ft

Sarcococca hookeriana* var. *digyna E: ◐
Suckering shrub with glossy dark green leaves. Useful for shade and for the intensely fragrant but insignificant flowers in late winter. 75cm × 1m/2½ × 3ft

Viburnum davidii E: ◐
Shrub of fine architectural form making a mound of glossy, dark green leaves. Turquoise-blue, egg-shaped fruits in autumn (following small white flowers in summer) if a small group are planted together to ensure cross-pollination. 1 × 1.5m/3 × 5ft

Plants for Difficult Spots

All gardens have troublesome areas where few plants will thrive, and these problems tend to occur in concentrated numbers near the house. The difficulty may be darkness caused by neighbouring buildings which block out the light, or it might be the sort of dry shade cast by a tree. Dankness as well as darkness is possible, perhaps in a gloomy corner where the house guttering drips. The converse of this type of problem is equally challenging where, for example, a terrace is simply an unshaded stone waste which cooks in summer. And arguably the worst problem of all is caused by a burial mound of rubble and hardcore which has been used in the construction of house or terrace. This proves to be usually a tomb for plants as well.

Short of drastic overhaul, the most sensible way of dealing with such problem areas is to place here only those plants which will endure these particular conditions. More vulnerable plants will be doomed.

Ferns are invaluable here, like the evergreen hart's tongue fern (*Asplenium scolopendrium*) with shining green fronds. It has crested variants. 40 × 30cm/1ft 4in × 1ft

***Gentiana asclepiadea* (Willow gentian)**
Graceful plant with Oxford blue (or white in the form 'Alba') tubular flowers in late summer–early autumn. It requires peaty soil. 60 × 30cm/2 × 1ft

Omphalodes cappadocica
A quickly running plant with bright blue small flowers in spring. 15 × 30cm/ 6in × 1ft

***Primula vulgaris* (Primrose)**
The common primrose produces a succession of pale lemon flowers in early spring. 7.5 × 15cm/3 × 6in

Smilacina racemosa LH
Sprays of creamy flowers in spring over arching foliage. This elegant perennial needs moist leafy soil. 75 × 45cm/2½ × 1½ft

Vinca (Periwinkle) E
These sub-shrubs make spring-flowering ground-cover, suited to banks. *V. major* (45cm/1½ft H and W) is the rampant form. *V. minor* (22 × 30cm/9in × 1ft) has smaller leaves. Both have variegated forms. Spring flowers of blue, white or garnet.

CONSIDER ALSO:

Ajuga p.104
Astilbe p.161
Astrantia carniolica p.161
Epimedium p.104
Heuchera p.175
Hosta in variety
Milium effusum 'Aureum' p.61
Primula japonica
P. pulverulenta p.186
Pulmonaria p.137
Tellima grandiflora p.105
Tiarella cordifolia
Viola in variety

Euphorbia cyparissias
Stems with grey-green leaves look like squirrels' tails. Lime-yellow flower-heads in early summer, on a running plant that makes invasive but good ground-cover. 25 × 30cm+/10in × 1ft+

Digitalis purpurea E
The Excelsior foxglove has most impact with 1.5m/5ft spikes; flowers of white, pink, apricot, primrose or purple. *D. lutea* is shorter with yellow flowers. *D.* × *mertonensis* is purplish pink; 75cm/2½ft. Summer-blooming, short-lived perennials or biennials for light soil. × 30cm/1ft

Epimedium* × *perralchicum E
A ground-cover plant with glossy green leaves and sprays of spurred yellow flowers in spring. 45cm/1½ft H and W

***Helleborus foetidus* (Stinking hellebore)**
Dark green fingered leaves with maroon-rimmed ice-green flower bells opening in early spring and lasting for a long period. 45cm/1½ft H and W

***Iris foetidissima* (Gladwin iris)** E
Broad leaves and quiet lilac or yellow flowers in summer, showy orange-scarlet seed-pods in autumn. 45cm/1½ft H and W

***Lamium galeobdolon* 'Florentinum'** (syn. 'Variegatum') E
A ground-coverer of the nettle family. Silver and dark green foliage; pale yellow flowers in early summer. Rampant. 30cm/1ft × indefinite

CONSIDER ALSO:

Alchemilla mollis p.52
Asperula odorata
Bergenia p.52
Euphorbia robbiae p.215
Millium effusum 'Aureum' p.61
Polygonatum × hybridum p.219
Tellima grandiflora p.105
Tiarella cordifolia
Viola labradorica p.91

CONSIDER ALSO:

Acanthus spinosus p.54
Allium in variety
Armeria p.94
Anthemis cupaniana p.214
Cerastium p.98
Cynara p.56
Eryngium in variety
Festuca glauca p.69
Foeniculum p.189
Gypsophila p.34
Linum in variety
Onopordum p.57
Othonna cheirifolia p.99
Phlomis fruticosa
Sisyrinchium striatum p.165
Thyme p.95
Verbascum
Yucca p.57
Also all plants on pp. 68–73 (Grey and Silver Plants) which are distinguished by the sign ❍.

***Cistus* × *pulverulentus* *'Sunset'* (Sun rose)** E: ❍
Compact shrub with grey-green leaves and magenta flowers produced prolifically in summer. Not fully hardy. 1m/3ft H and W. All other cistus are also suited to this position.

***Helianthemum* 'Wisley Primrose' (Sun rose)** E: O
Lemon yellow flowers over grey-green leaves on this single-flowered form. The individual flowers are fleeting but there is a prolonged display. All helianthemums are likewise suited to this position. 25 × 45cm/10in × 1½ft

Iris germanica ❍
The bearded iris needs its rhizomes baked by sun. The colour range includes white, green, yellow, bronze, pink, carmine, wine, pale to deep blue, lavender to purple as well as bicolours. 60cm–1.2m × 30cm/2–4 × 1ft

Dutch iris
A hybrid of *I. xiphium* and related species, the Dutch iris provides an easy, glamorous show in early summer. The colour range includes blue and gold. 60 × 10cm/2ft × 4in

***Rosmarinus* (Rosemary)** E: ❍
The aromatic, grey-green leafed shrub, for culinary as well as ornamental use. Small blue flowers in spring, at their brightest in the shrub 'Severn Sea'. There is also an erect-growing form called 'Fastigiatus' or 'Miss Jessop's Variety'. The ordinary rosemary (*Rosmarinus officinalis*) reaches about 1.2 × 1m/ 4 × 3ft.

***Salvia officinalis* (Sage)** E: ❍
The best foliage forms of this shrubby sage are the purple-leafed 'Purpurascens', shown above, the variegated green and gold 'Icterina', and 'Tricolor' with its grey-green leaves marked with white, pink and purple. Spikes of blue-purple flowers in summer.

Senecio leucostachys E: ❍
Filigree, silvery white leaves on stems which intermesh with shrubs or a wall trellis. Small white flowers in summer. Tender. 60cm (more in mild winter areas) × 45cm/2 × 1½ft

Dianthus gratianopolitanus E: ❍
The Cheddar pink with its pink flowers and cushion of leaves is easy and usually naturalizes. It bears very fragrant blooms in midsummer. 15cm/6in H and W

Centranthus ruber **(Valerian)**
Maroon, rose or white flower-sprays on a plant which often naturalizes in walls. Self-sowing and invasive. A beautiful plant but its seed-heads need to be cut off if it is to be controlled.
60 × 45cm/2 × 1½ft

Mesembryanthemum **(Livingstone daisy)** E: ❍
A large family of mostly trailing succulents with rayed flowers blooming all summer in a brilliant colour range. They need sun to thrive and complete winter cover as all are tender. 15 × 30cm/6in × 1ft

Nasturtium (*Tropaeolum majus*) ❍
Frost-tender, but will flower summer through till late autumn on gritty soil if it is not too poor. It is obtainable in shades of red, yellow or orange, and with plain green or marbled green and cream leaves. Single or double flowers. 15 × 45cm/6in × 1½ft

***Sedum album tenuifolium murale* (Wall sedum)** E: ❍
Invasively self-sowing though useful in the right position, this little white flowered succulent will spill down steps or in paving. 10 × 15cm/4 × 6in

***Sempervivum* 'Commander Hay'** E: ❍
A cultivar with large rosy rosettes and pink flowers in summer. 20cm/8in H and W. Almost all the houseleek varieties will adapt to these conditions.

The Four Seasons

The best gardens remain beautiful at all seasons. Not an easy requirement, so it has to be planned. As each new season replaces the last, the appearance of the garden changes and gives a succession of new pleasures. Glistening berries follow flowers, autumn blossom takes over from summer which has succeeded spring. And in a well-planned garden, even winter brings its choice flowers, scents and fruits.

Shrubs for Seasonal Display

Whether you are planting a mixed or a shrub border, it is a good idea to ensure some continuity of flowering throughout the year. A selection of flowers for winter is given on pages 138–9 but here is a choice of some of the best flowering shrubs for a spring to autumn display. They represent a possible nucleus to which you can add shrubs from the rest of the book. You might decide to confine yourself to different representatives of just one (or two) genus for a particular season. If so, arguably the best for spring are camellias; for midsummer and after, roses (with cistus quite a good second in mild-winter areas, even though they are not reliably hardy nor as long-lived); for later summer and into autumn, hydrangeas. These groups alone will given you an enormous choice of cultivars.

Berberis darwinii E
Clustered orange flowers followed by dusky blue fruits on a large, prickly weed-suppressing shrub, growing to 4m/13ft H and W.

Forsythia* × *intermedia
A vigorous shrub which makes a very showy display early in the year, which makes up for its rather dull green foliage. One of the best cultivars is 'Lynwood'. 3 × 1.8m/ 10 × 6ft

***Camellia* × *williamsii* 'Galaxie'** E: LH:◐
This bushy shrub with glossy dark green leaves is arguably one of the most floriferous of all the camellias. It makes twiggy growth which is festooned with masses of soft pink flowers, veined with a deeper rose. It is a manageable choice for a small garden. 1.5 × 1.2m/5 × 4ft

***Magnolia liliiflora* 'Nigra'**
LH: ○
Dark wine-red flowers like huge elongated tulips bloom from mid-spring to midsummer and sometimes recurrently later. It forms a compact hardy shrub of 4 × 3m/ 13 × 10ft.

***Magnolia stellata* (Star magnolia)**
White many-petalled starry flowers cover the shrub in early spring. It is not vigorous but a valuable lime-tolerant magnolia. 3 × 4m/10 × 13ft

***Spiraea* × *arguta* (Bridal veil)**
The most elegant of the spiraeas with arching growth, festooned with white flowers. 2.4m/8ft H and W

Viburnum* × *juddii
Very sweetly scented flowers which are pink in bud, white when open, bloom freely from mid to late spring. 1.5m/5ft H and W

***Rhododendron* 'Golden Torch'** E: LH: ◐
This Yakushimanum hybrid makes a dome-forming evergreen shrub which is covered in soft pinky-cream clusters of open flowers in mid-spring. 1m/ 3ft H and W

***Rhododendron* 'Praecox'** Semi-E: LH: ◐
This shrub blooms very early in spring when its delicate rosy-purple flowers are freely produced. 1.2 × 1m/4 × 3ft

CONSIDER ALSO:
Ceanothus (spring-flowering forms in variety)
Magnolia × *soulangeana*

***Cistus* × *cyprius* (Sun rose)** E: ❍
A good example of a group of beautiful but often slightly tender shrubs, all requiring full sun, light soil and no manure. This is one of the hardiest with white flowers with a deep maroon central blotch and leaden green leaves.
1.8 × 1.2m/6 × 4ft

Cistus* × *purpureus E: ❍
This sun rose is not fully hardy but worth growing in a sheltered position for its long, magnificent display of deep rose flowers with maroon blotches and soft grey-green foliage. Bushy growth to 1.5 × 1.8m/5 × 6ft

CONSIDER ALSO:

Carpenteria californica p.50
Cistus 'Peggy Sammons' p.51
Cistus × *pulverulentus*
Paeonia delavayi p.29
P.d. var. *ludlowii* p.181
Roses on pages 78–9, 224–5

***Paeonia suffruticosa* (Tree peony)** ❍
A glorious shrub of which there are many named forms. This is 'Sitifukujin', a Japanese cultivar, with huge golden-bossed rose blooms and glaucous foliage. Shade from morning sun. 1.2 × 1.5m/4 × 5ft

Rose ❍
A vast genus, but the most useful roses for the border are either the repeat-flowering shrub roses, or reasonably disease-resistant cultivars of the floribunda roses, or else a selected few of those roses that supply a fine display of autumn fruit after blooming. Of the first group we show here an old Hybrid Musk shrub rose, 'Cornelia' with clusters of small, pink, salmon-flushed flowers from early summer to autumn. 1.8 × 2.1m/6 × 7ft

'Golden Wings' is one of the most elegant of the modern shrub roses, a large single yellow in continuous bloom, growing to 1.2m/4ft H and W.

Floribunda or cluster-flowered roses produce their blooms almost continuously from summer to autumn. 'Amber Queen' is a very fragrant example with neat bushy growth. 60cm/2ft H and W

The fruiting category of roses is represented here by 'Frau Dagmar Hastrup', a healthy Rugosa rose with large, single pink flowers from early to late summer, followed by crimson heps. 1.5m/5ft H and W

Deutzia setchuenensis corymbiflora
Most of the deutzias are pretty, early-summer-flowering shrubs, but this is arguably the most elegant and more valuable for its blooms in the second half of the summer. Starry white flowers in corymbs. Not fully hardy. 1.5 × 1m/5 × 3ft

Hydrangea 'Blue Wave' ◐
One of a group of hardy shrubs making a fine display in summer to mid-autumn. This form is a vigorous lace-cap growing to 1.8 × 2.1m/6 × 7ft. Lime-free soil is necessary to ensure blue flowers; slightly limy soil will produce pink or red flowers; very alkaline soils are unsuitable.

***Fuchsia* 'Margaret'**
Fuchsias bloom continuously from summer until frosts. This is a vigorous bushy form with rich deep pink sepals and a violet corolla. It is not fully hardy. Don't cut off the top growth, which may have died in the winter, until the spring. 1.4 × 1m/4 × 3ft

Hydrangea paniculata
A lovely shrub flowering from late summer to early autumn with long panicles of fertile and sterile florets. In the form 'Grandiflora' the inflorescence is up to 30cm/1ft long. For moist rich soil. 2.7 × 2.1m/9 × 7ft

***Hydrangea quercifolia* (Oak-leafed hydrangea)** ◐
This variety has pendent, cream, lacy panicles in midsummer to autumn. Its bold foliage, cut like that of an oak, often colours richly in autumn. 1.5 × 2.1m/5 × 7ft

CONSIDER ALSO:

Buddleja davidii p.180
Fuchsias in variety
Hebe in variety on page 107
Hydrangea villosa

***Acer palmatum* 'Atropurpureum'**
A Japanese maple with finely cut bronzy purple foliage which turns brilliant red in the autumn. It needs protection from strong sun and cold winds. 4.5m/15ft H and W

Fothergilla major LH
White, bottle-brush flower-spikes in spring, and flame and yellow autumn foliage make this a dual-season shrub. Peaty, lime-free soil. 3m/10ft H and W

Enkianthus campanulatus
LH: ◐
Pale buff, pendent bell-flowers in clusters in early summer, a tiered-branch habit and rich autumn foliage. Peaty, lime-free soil, part-shade. 3m/10ft H and W

Euonymus alatus
This is a slow-growing shrub with a spreading habit. The leaves turn a rich and deepening red in the autumn. 3/10ft H and W

***Rhus typhina* 'Laciniata'**
(syn. 'Dissecta') ❍
The cut-leafed female cultivar of the popular stag's-horn sumach provides rich autumn colour. Conical fruits persisting in winter. 2.7 × 4.5m/9 × 15ft

Callicarpa bodinieri var. ***geraldii*** ❍
A shrub that produces extraordinary small violet berries in the autumn when the foliage also turns mauve. Plant several bushes together to ensure satisfactory pollination. 2.1 × 1.8m/7 × 6ft

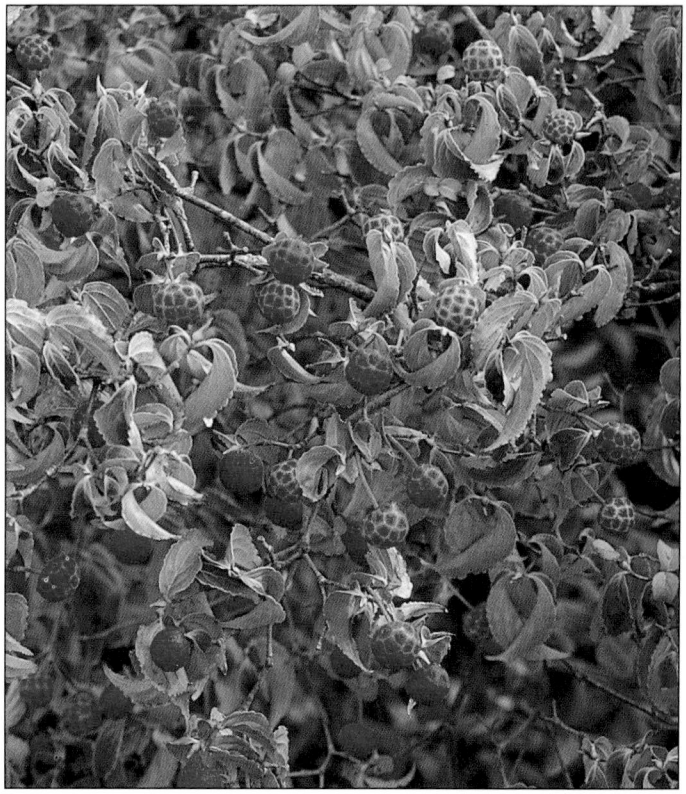

Cornus kousa var. ***chinensis*** **(Chinese dogwood)**
A shrub with a dual display of wonderful white 'flowers' (bracts) in summer followed by strawberry-like fruits. 3.6 × 4m/12 × 13ft

Cotoneaster salicifolius **'Exburyensis'** E
An arching graceful hybrid shrub with bunches of small yellow fruits in autumn that persist on the branches. 5m/16ft H and W

***Rosa moyesii* 'Geranium'**
Single scarlet flowers in early summer followed by large, red, bottle-shaped autumn fruits. Bushy, erect growth.
2.4 × 2.1m/8 × 7ft

***Viburnum opulus* 'Xanthocarpum'**
A vigorous and healthy form of the guelder rose with golden translucent berries in autumn following on from the white lace-cap flowers.
4m/13ft H and W

Skimmia japonica E: ◐
The females berry if pollinated by a male. The best combination is the female cultivar 'Foremanii' which produces abundant berries, planted with the male 'Fragrans' with its scented, creamy flower spikes in early summer. Both are evergreen and better in part-shade.
1 × 1.5m/3 × 5ft

CONSIDER ALSO:

Arbutus unedo p.244
Cotoneaster frigidus 'Cornubia' p.244
Malus 'Evereste' p.244
Pernettya (Gaultheria) mucronata p.109
Pyracantha in variety p.198

Bulbs, Corms etc through the Year

Bulbs are the ideal subject for a small area, because they will give colour in the minimum space and in return for minimum effort. Also they can be chosen to give flowers each month of the year, even in winter when little else is in bloom. Plant them where they will suffer the least disturbance. Strong-growing bulbs are suitable between herbaceous plants and deciduous shrubs, even at the foot of deciduous trees if they do not demand a sunny, open position. Small, choice and difficult bulbs will probably need planting in a separate area, lest they are swamped by their ranker neighbours. Tender subjects which require a summer baking can be placed at the foot of sunny walls where they can act as a sumptuous carpet for climbers. Stiff, upright bulbs like hybrid tulips which need to be lifted each year are suited to formal open-ground displays. Species bulbs which will naturalize are most appealing when scattered in groups of informal appearance.

Anemone nemorosa ◐
A single, white or lilac-flushed flower in the wild form, good for naturalizing; though near a house, the double white form (shown here) or one of the single pale blue cultivars or lavender 'Allenii' is more suitable. 15cm/6in

Anemone blanda
This wind flower is sun-loving and spreading on light soil; white, blue, pink or deep rose in the form 'Radar'. It is fully hardy but as it blooms at a chilly time of the year, will benefit from a sheltered spot. 8cm/3in

***Erythronium* 'White Beauty' ◐**
Exquisite bulb for cool leafy soil which does not dry out. 25cm/10in. Other fine hybrids include the lemon 'Kondo' and yellow 'Pagoda' both with marbled leaves.

Chionodoxa luciliae
Blue (or pink or white) stars on a bulb spreading invasively in light soil, forming mass colour. 8cm/3in

***Fritillaria meleagris* 'Aphrodite'**
White form of the snake's head fritillary, the type plant bearing bells with a plum-red chequer pattern, also shown. For moist soil, sun or light shade. 25cm/10in

Fritillaria imperialis
The yellow or rusty-red crown imperial needs sun and well-drained soil; it has a pungent smell and is one of the most distinctive bulbs one can grow. In heavy soils the bulb can be planted slightly on its side, or sand/grit added to the earth. 1m/3ft

***Narcissus* 'Thalia'**
This is one of the best white trumpet daffodils (30cm/1ft) though the slightly larger 'Mount Hood' surpasses it for naturalizing.

For further tulips see page 211.

Leucojum aestivum
Flourishing in moist soil, 'Gravetye Giant' is the finest form of the snowflake. Up to 60cm/2ft

***Tulipa kaufmanniana* 'Gaiety'** ❍
A vigorous cultivar which flowers in early spring. 20cm/8in

Tulips ❍
Of the numerous hybrids, 'Burgundy' is one of the richest coloured of the lily-flowering cultivars, which are fairly resistant to bad weather. All this group have flowers of elegant form. 45cm/1½ft

CONSIDER ALSO:

Crocosmia in variety
Zantedeschia aethiopica 'Crowborough' p.187

Allium aflatunense ❍
A handsome ornamental onion flowering in early summer. There is also a darker striking variant called 'Purple Sensation'. 75cm/2½ft

Allium christophii ❍
One of the most dazzling onions with huge starry lilac heads on a 40cm/1ft 4in stem in summer. Good for drying. The handsome architecturally formed heads and stems will last for years when dried.

Camassia leichtlinii
Easy in heavy, rather moist soils, with white or blue flowers. The plants have untidy leaves which die down soon after flowering. 75cm+/2½ft+

Galtonia candicans ❍
Strap-like leaves and ivory, sometimes green-tipped bells on 1m/3ft stems (seen here in front of grey-stemmed verbascums). For well drained but moist soil.

Gladiolus* × *colvillei (syn *nanus*) ❍
Delicately pretty and long-flowering, peach-pink, white or orange cultivars, with contrastingly pale and dark throats. For light soil; not always hardy.
30–45cm/1–1½ft

Lilium candidum ❍
The fragrant madonna lily, needing sun, a heavy soil and no disturbance. The basal leaves appear in autumn and persist through the winter. 1.2m/4ft

Lilium martagon ◐
With pink-purple or white flowers for semi-shade and leafy soil where it will naturalize.
60cm–1.2m/2–4ft

***Lilium* 'Stargazer'** ❍
A magnificent and fragrant lily which is suitable for a pot or in the garden. The flowers open on 1m/3ft stems. It is a very showy cultivar and a good garden plant.

***Colchicum autumnale* (Autumn crocus)**
There are white forms of this bulb, and also double as well as single, but all bloom in autumn when the plant is leafless. The following spring a sheaf of large leaves appears before dying away. Up to 15cm/6in

***Crinum* × *powellii* ❍**
Magnificent pale to deep pink or white flowers on a tall stem above spreading strap-shaped leaves. In cold areas, will do best at the foot of a hot wall where it may need watering to induce free-flowering. Protect in harsh winters. 1m/3ft

***Schizostylis* 'Sunrise' ❍**
A good pink form of the Kaffir lily. *S. coccinea* is crimson red. They need full sun and well-drained though not dry soil. Not fully hardy. 60cm/2ft

***Nerine bowdenii* ❍**
Valuable bulb for its late, glistening pink flowers, freely produced. 'Fenwick's Variety' is slightly taller with larger flowers. For well-drained soil. Not fully hardy. 45–60cm/1½–2ft

Crocus in variety
C. tommasinianus, lavender in the type, though shown here in its deep form, 'Whitewell Purple' is a pretty though sometimes invasively self-sowing variety for winter or earliest spring. *C. chrysanthus*, especially in its rich blue forms like 'Bluebird', 'Blue Pearl' or 'Zenith' is also beautiful. 7.5cm/3in

Cyclamen hederifolium (syn. *C. neapolitanum*) ◐
This pretty cyclamen produces its rose or white flowers in autumn above silver-marbled leaves. It will self-sow and gradually produce a carpet of blossom. 7.5cm/3in

Eranthis hyemalis
Where happy, the winter aconite will spread into a carpet of bright gold, green-ruffed flowers. 7.5cm/3in

CONSIDER ALSO:
Winter-flowering bulbs, p. 136
Bulbs for the foot of hedges, pp. 210–11

Galanthus nivalis
The snowdrop has many variants, including double forms but the ordinary single type is the best for naturalizing. 10cm/4in

Iris unguicularis (syn. *I. stylosa*) E: ❍
A winter-flowering rhizomatous perennial available in white or lavender forms of which 'Mary Barnard' is the deepest colour. Good drainage is necessary. 30cm/1ft

Winter Flowers

A problem common to all gardens in cold climates is how to keep them attractive and inviting throughout winter. One solution is to include a high proportion of evergreens amongst the plants. The other answer is to establish a fair number of winter-flowering subjects. Admittedly the amount of plants that bloom reliably in winter is minuscule compared with their spring and summer counterparts, but the actual range is nonetheless wide and includes bulbs, herbaceous plants, small and large shrubs. Plant the small subjects in strong clusters, spaced at intervals so that their presence can be seen at a distance and so that they enliven a greater area of the garden.

Supplement the list below with the winter flowering bulbs on page 135, the brightly-coloured evergreens on pages 60–7, and some of the bolder-leafed evergreens on pages 52–9.

Cyclamen coum ◐
This small bulb flowers in winter or earliest spring. There are white or magenta forms, both with plain dark green leaves. 7.5cm/3in

***Iris reticulata* 'Harmony'** ○
This kind of iris will give a dependable annual show in late winter/early spring if the bulb is planted in moist but well drained conditions. 10cm/4in

Narcissus bulbocodium ○
The yellow hoop-petticoat narcissi are spring charmers, one of the earliest and best being the soft lemon *N.b. romieuxii* in mid-winter. Good drainage is essential. 12.5cm/5in

Narcissus cyclamineus
Charming small daffodil with a long trumpet and completely swept-back petals in early spring. For acid soils. 15cm/6in

Scilla mischtschenkoana (syn. *tubergeniana*) ◐
In very early spring, each bulb produces about three flower spikes, the silver blue petals marked with darker blue veins. A good naturalizer. 10cm/4in

Viola odorata E
The sweet violet can be in bloom from February on. Wine-red, white, pink and yellow cultivars as well as violet. Its green leaves form a spreading carpet. 10 × 30cm/4in × 1ft

Helleborus orientalis E: ◐
The most invaluable of all late winter/early spring flowers. A huge range of shades is obtainable from white to deepest black, all with handsome divided foliage. Other valuable hellebores include *H. foetidus* (p.113) and *H. argutifolius* (p.53). 30–45 × 45cm/1–1½ × 1½ft

Pulmonaria **(Lungwort)** ◐
The earliest to bloom is *P. rubra* in late winter with plain green leaves and coral-red flowers, followed by a succession of different lungworts. 'Sissinghurst White', above, is a particularly pretty one for early spring. All 15–30 × 30cm/6in–1ft × 1ft

***Chimonanthus praecox* (Winter Sweet)** ❍
Very fragrant pale yellow flowers, stained purple, rather larger in the cultivar 'Grandiflorus'. Give it a sunny wall. 2.5m/8ft H and W

Clematis cirrhosa* var. *balearica E:❍
Give this climber a sheltered wall for its flowers which appear from mid-winter onwards. Finely-cut leaves and pale green, nodding blooms with red spots within. Up to 4m/13ft

***Camellia* 'Nobilissima'** E: LH: ◐
One of the earliest of the *C. japonica* hybrids with large snowy blossoms in late winter/early spring. These turn buff before falling. *C. sasanqua* 'Narumigata' is a true winter flowerer, opening its white flowers from carmine buds in early winter but it is not fully hardy. Both are best on a wall that avoids early sun which will blight the flowers if they are frosted. 3m/10ft H and W

Corylopsis pauciflora LH: ◐
Small fragrant pale yellow bells hang along the branches in early spring of this bushy shrub. The leaves are bronze when first emerging before greening. 1.5m/5ft H and W

Daphne mezereum ❍
Scented reddish purple flowers (or white in the variety 'Alba') cluster along the stems in late winter or earliest spring. 1m/3ft H and W

***Daphne odora* 'Aureomarginata'** E: ❍
A shapely bush which needs a sunny sheltered position, with cream-bordered evergreen leaves and intensely fragrant flowers in small clusters in earliest spring. 1 × 1.5m/ 3 × 5ft

***Hamamelis* × *intermedia* 'Pallida'** LH
One of the loveliest Chinese witch-hazels with spreading branches massed in late winter onwards with pale yellow flowers. Bold leaves. 4m/13ft H and W

Jasminum nudiflorum
A shrub best trained on a wall to control its long, green, trailing stems. Wonderful show of yellow flowers throughout late autumn to early spring. 3m/10ft H and W

CONSIDER ALSO:
Erica × *darleyensis* p.107
Viburnum × *bodnantense* 'Dawn', p.77

***Rhododendron* 'Bric-a-Brac'** E: LH: ◐
A lovely and floriferous hybrid which flowers in late winter to early spring. Its flowers are vulnerable to frosts and it benefits from a sheltered position. For moist woodland soil. 1.5m/5ft H and W

Rhododendron moupinense E: LH: ◐
Species with white, pale or dark pink flowers (sometimes freckled) blooming in late winter/early spring. It needs peaty soil and part shade. 1m/3ft H and W

Long-season Flowers

Many flowering plants remain in bloom for only a short period, varying from a few days to several weeks. This is acceptable when they are chosen primarily for their foliage or are planted in a garden which is spacious enough to contain many different varieties ensuring successional blossom throughout the seasons. It is less welcome on a terrace or in a very small garden where space is at a premium. In this situation, one needs flowers which remain in beauty for a long while or are produced continuously over an extended period.

Campanula portenschlagiana (syn. *muralis*) E
Trailing bellflower with purplish blue flowers all summer. 10 × 45cm/4in × 1½ft. Some of the dwarf hybrids have an equally prolonged display like the lavender 'Birch Hybrid' (see page 100) or 'Stella', a form of *C. poscharskyana*.

***Dianthus* 'Doris' (Pink)** E: ❍
With its salmon-pink flowers and silvery leaves this hybrid blooms all summer. It is a cultivar of the *Dianthus allwoodii* group, short-lived but in perpetual bloom. 30cm/1ft H and W

Diascia vigilis ❍
Showy warm pink flowers in summer cover the upright spikes of a valuable though not fully hardy perennial. 30–45 × 60cm/1–1½ × 2ft

Geranium sanguineum* var. *striatum ❍
Pink flowers cover wide mounds of leaves from early summer till winter. There is also a white form called 'Album'. The type is magenta. 30 × 45cm/1 × 1½ft

Polyanthus
Individual blooms may be spoilt by wind and rain early in the year. Wine, scarlet, pink, bronze, orange, yellow, white, blue and violet forms can be raised from seed. 10 × 15cm/8 × 6in

***Osteospermum ecklonis* (African daisy)** ❍
All osteospermums give a long display. This variety has dark-centred shining white flowers produced en masse from early summer until autumn frosts. A wonderful display but the plant is not fully hardy and needs good drainage. 30 × 45cm/1 × 1½ft

***Primula auricula* (Auricula)**
Flowers are carried in spring to early summer above soft green leaves. A wide range of colour and some varieties are dusted with a white farina. 15cm/6in H and W

***Primula* 'Guinevere'**
With its bronzed leaves and yellow-eyed lilac flowers this is amongst the most distinct primrose cultivars. But there is a huge range amongst the primroses, both vivid and subtle, and including laced petals and contrasting speckling. 15cm/6in H and W

Viola cornuta E
This viola will flower from spring until frosts, especially the white form, 'Alba', or the blue form, 'Lilacina'. Other long-flowering violas include 'Bowles' Black', the darkest; 'Irish Molly', lime-green and red; 'Jackanapes', a yellow and mahogany bloom. 12 × 15cm/5 × 6in

Anemone* × *hybrida (syn. *A. japonica*)
Graceful and indispensable flowers which bloom from late summer to autumn. There are both double and single forms, white or pink. 75 × 45cm/2½ × 1½ft. The form 'September Charm' is shorter at 45cm/1½ft.

***Campanula persicifolia* 'Telham Beauty' (Peach-leafed bellflower)** E: ❍
Blue cups all summer on an easy plant, though best in light soil. There is a white form, self-sowing, like the blue type plant. 1m × 30cm/3 × 1ft

Coreopsis verticillata ❍
A reliable and clump-forming spreader with delicate foliage and an unending succession of dazzling golden daisy flowers throughout the summer. 60 × 45cm/ 2 × 1½ft

***Fuchsia* 'Lena'**
Fairly hardy pink and purple cultivar in continuous bloom from summer until frosts. 60 × 45cm/2 × 1½ft. In mild districts the plants will grow large as they are shrubs; in cold districts, they will be cut to the ground each winter and live the life of herbaceous plants.

Penstemon ❍
Sub-shrubs for well-drained, fertile soil. Not all are hardy but 'Garnet', a dark red, is fairly reliable. White, red and purple cultivars are obtainable. 'Cherry Ripe' and the scarlet 'Firebird' are forms of *P. hartwegii* which flower from summer till autumn. 60 × 45cm/2 × 1½ft

CONSIDER ALSO:

Aster × frikartii p.161
Centaurea hypoleuca 'John Coutts' p.161
Dahlia p.170
Dianthus deltoides p.96
Salvia × superba p.165
Many annual and half-hardy annuals are also suitable, including *Begonia semperflorens*, Cleome, *Cosmos*, Nasturtium, *Impatiens* (busy lizzie), *Nicotiana* and *Verbena*.
See also the long-season annuals shown on pages 154–5.

***Tradescantia virginiana* 'Purple Dome' (Spiderwort)**
Three-petalled flowers all summer till frosts. Varieties include white with a blue centre in the form 'Osprey', violet-blue in 'Isis', mauve-blue in 'J.C. Weguelin'. 45cm/1½ft H and W

***Linum narbonense* 'Heavenly Blue'** ❍
Intense sky-blue flowers all summer on wiry stems. Group for a brilliant display. Best on rich, light soils, but even in these conditions the plant tends to be short-lived. 45 × 30cm/1½ × 1ft

Hydrangea in variety ◐
Examples include *H. serrata* 'Grayswood' (above left), a neat shrub to 1.2m/4ft H and W, its blue and white lace-caps changing from white to pink in summer and finally deep crimson in autumn; or 'Preziosa' with domed pink heads ageing to claret: 1.5m/5ft H and W. Of the mop-heads, *H. macrophylla* 'Hamburg' (above right) with rosy florets has a long season. 1.8 × 2.4m/6 × 8ft

***Lavatera* 'Barnsley'** ○
Fast growing with palest pink flowers all summer and downy leaves. Not fully hardy and best in well-drained, poorish soil to stop any tendency to run to leaf. 1.8m/6ft H and W

***Potentilla fruticosa* 'Elizabeth'**
Primrose flowers over a dense mound from late spring until frosts. 1m/3ft H and W. 'Tangerine' is rich orange; 'Red Ace' is the closest to red. 'Abbotswood' is white.

Romneya coulteri ❍
Large white flowers with golden stamens from summer onwards, and grey-green leaves. It can be difficult to establish, but where happy, it can invade a border. 1.5/5ft × indefinite spread

Roses: Floribunda ❍
The Floribunda group contains some of the most floriferous and perpetual roses such as 'Escapade' (above) with fragrant, white-centred rosy-lilac flowers. Vigorous, bushy and healthy. 1.2m/4ft H and W. Consider also 'Amber Queen', a beautiful Floribunda, shown on p. 123.

Floribundas were preceded by Polyantha Pompons, smaller but with continuity of bloom also; of these 'Natalie Nypels' (above) has semi-double, fragrant pink flowers till winter. 1m/3ft H and W

English roses combine the repeat-flowering habit of modern-bush roses with the sumptuous, many-petalled flowers of the old roses. 'Sweet Juliet' (above) is a very fragrant example with a strong upright leafy habit. 1.2 × 1m/4 × 3ft

***Clematis* 'Jackmanii Superba'**
Velvety purple flowers, larger than those on the usual × *jackmanii* plant are produced prolifically from summer to early autumn. Up to 6m/20ft. See also clematis on pp. 222–3.

***Eccremocarpus scaber* ❍**
Fast-growing plant but not reliably hardy. Little orange-red (or yellow) tubular flowers all summer till frost. Bi-pinnate leaves on stems to 4.5m. Easy from seed.

***Jasminum officinale* ❍**
Small, fragrant white flowers in clusters all summer. Green or variegated leaves on a popular old climber that prefers sun but tolerates almost any soil. Vigorous to 7m/23ft

***Rosa* 'Golden Showers'**
This rose tolerates part-shaded walls and has a long season, bearing bright yellow semi-double flowers fading to cream. 3m/10ft
Consider also *R.* 'Mermaid' on p. 224.

Other long-flowering shrubs and climbers include:

Cobaea scandens p.150
Fremontodendron 'California Glory' p.222
Hydrangea arborescens 'Grandiflora' p.201
Ipomoea p.150
Thunbergia alata p.150

***Rosa* 'Climbing Iceberg'** ❍
Few climbing roses can be termed fully perpetual, but this climbing form of the floribunda, provides recurrent flushes of its white flowers over glossy pale green leaves from early summer to autumn. 4m/13ft

Temporary Effects: Annuals, Pots etc.

In any confined space, one needs a change of plants to avoid the monotony of looking at the same scene day after day. Annuals and half-hardy annuals are temporary residents and will give an abundance of flower and/or lushness of foliage that only the warm weather makes possible.

The most useful are those annuals with a long season in flower and also those plants which perform well in pots and tubs. Plant annuals in bare pockets or areas, or sow the longer-flowering varieties in the empty spaces of any missing paving stones, so long as the soil is friable. Consider also using tender, rapid-growing climbers either to fill spaces on walls or to festoon large shrubs or to conceal structural eyesores etc. before permanent plants have begun to cover them.

Most annuals will flourish only in full sun, but a few in the lists on these pages will thrive in shadier positions.

Cobaea scandens ❍
Tender perennial grown as a half-hardy annual. Purple bells or cream in the form 'Alba'. Gives dense coverage, but needs support. May sprint to 6m/20ft in the season.

Ipomoea rubro caerulea ❍
This is the blue morning glory. Other forms have deep violet, carmine or white flowers, or striped or variegated blooms or leaves. Grown as a half-hardy annual, but blooms well only in warm summers. Support is necessary. 3m/10ft

Lathyrus odoratus **(Sweet pea)** ❍
There is a large colour range of this hardy annual, including bi-colours. All are fragrant. The antique varieties are even more scented but tend to have small flowers and an untidy habit of growth. 1.8m/6ft

Nasturtium (*Tropaeolum*) ❍
The climbing form flowers all summer in a range of yellows and reds. Will trail to give ground-cover or climb on a trellis, shrubs or a hedge. One of its virtues is that it will do well on poor, dry soil. Hardy annual. 1.8m/6ft

Thunbergia alata ❍
Thin climber with cream or orange flowers with a black centre, or white with a yellow centre in the form 'Angel Wings'. Blooms for a long period. Support with a wire trellis or canes, or use as a trailing plant in a container. Tender perennial grown as a half-hardy annual. May reach 2.4m/8ft.

Abutilon hybrids ❍
Shrubby plants which can be flowered as half-hardy annuals. Beautifully veined, open bell-flowers in cream, yellow, primrose, pink, scarlet or wine shades. Tender. 1m × 60cm/3 × 2ft

Agave americana E: ❍
Frost-tender succulent with a blue-grey rosette of leaves with fierce spines. *A.a.* 'Marginata' is shown here, a striking gold-variegated form. 45cm/1½ft H and W. Position the potted plants with caution to avoid injury, and better omit them altogether where there are children or pets.

Amaranthus caudatus **(Love-lies-bleeding)**
A distinctive hardy annual with trailing maroon (or green in the form 'Viridis') long flower tassels from late summer to autumn. Can self-sow. 60 × 45cm/ 2 × 1½ft

Datura (syn. *Brugmansia*) ***fastuosa*** (syn. *metel*) ❍
Large single or double, scented trumpets of white, violet or pale yellow on a tender, bushy plant to 1m × 60cm/3 × 2ft. Can be flowered as half-hardy annual. The white and fragrant *D. suaveolens* shown here is impressive grown as a standard for a big tub. All are poisonous. 1.8 × 1m/6 × 3ft

***Heliotropium peruvianum* (Cherry pie)** ❍
This tender perennial is very strongly perfumed. It looks well in a pot positioned against silver foliage. 45cm/1½ft H and W

***Eucomis bicolor* (Pineapple plant)**
A spectacular bulb with long-lasting though initially unpleasantly smelling flowers in midsummer and attractive green seed-capsules. Not fully hardy. 45cm/1½ft

***Fuchsia* 'Thalia'**
A graceful tender fuchsia with tubular, red flowers. Very floriferous from summer through till autumn. 60cm/2ft H and W. Good tender hybrids include 'Dollar Princess' (rich purple corolla and crimson sepals), and 'Coachman' (deep salmon corolla, pink sepals).

***Pelargonium* 'Madame Layal' (Geranium)** ❍
A very pretty cultivar that belongs to the Angel group with distinctively zoned flowers like small pansies. A good small tender perennial for a pot. 30cm/1ft H and W

***Ricinus communis* (Castor-oil plant)** ❍
A tender perennial that is grown as a half-hardy annual. The form usually grown is 'Gibsonii' or 'Impala' with large bronzed leaves and small orange flower clusters. Poisonous seeds. 1.5 × 1m/5 × 3ft

***Asarina* 'Victoria Falls'** ❍
A tender tuberous perennial with soft green leaves and brilliant magenta trumpets which will cascade along its stems for most of the summer. Trailing to 45cm/1½ft

Helichrysum petiolare ❍
A tender grey-leafed perennial which is indispensable for a hanging basket. Its cool coloured foliage is a foil to brighter companions. To 45cm/1½ft

***Fuchsia* 'Pink Galore'**
A cascading shy-branching double fuchsia which is not too vigorous for a basket and will flower from summer to autumn. Trailing to 45cm/1½ft

Lotus berthelotii ❍
A spectacular silver filigree-leafed plant with scarlet claw flowers is an unusual and dramatic addition to a hanging basket. To 60cm/2ft

***Pelargonium* 'Roller's Pioneer' (Ivy-leafed geranium)** ❍
These tender perennials will tolerate drought as they are slightly succulent. This form has marbled-leaves, a marking that is called crocodile. Trailing to 60cm/2ft

Verbena ❍
There are several named varieties of which 'Sissinghurst' is one of the most popular with an unending succession of bright pink flowers from summer to autumn at the end of its trailing stems. To 40cm/1ft 4in

Begonia semperflorens
A fibrous-rooted begonia grown as a half-hardy annual, though a tender perennial. Colours include white, pink, scarlet or bi-colours and bronze or green foliage. Blooms all summer until frosts and will also tolerate shade. 15 × 20cm/6 × 8in

Anagallis monellii ❍
Gentian blue flowers with a red eye twinkle on a dwarf bushy tender perennial, usually grown as a half-hardy annual which flowers unendingly from summer until autumn. 15cm/6in H and W

***Antirrhinum* (Snapdragon)** ❍
Short-lived perennial best grown as a half-hardy annual. Single or double flowers in shades of yellow, orange, pink, scarlet, wine and white. 15cm–1m × 30cm/ 6in–3ft × 1ft

***Arctotis* hybrids (African daisy)** ❍
Bushy plants with daisy-flowers in shades of cream, yellow, pink or crimson. 45cm/1½ft H and W. Grown as half-hardy annuals.

Cosmos ❍
Graceful ferny-leafed plants with large single flowers of crimson, rose or white over a long season. Also gold or orange variety with two rows of petals growing to 75 × 30cm/2½ × 1ft.

Impatiens hybrids **(Busy Lizzie)**
A valuable tender perennial for moist sun or shade, blooming continuously all summer. Usually single flowers in red, white, mauve, orange or pink, though there is also a rose-like, double-flowered form in the same colour range. This will not tolerate full shade. 30cm–1m/1–3ft H and W

Osteospermum hybrids **(African daisy)** ❍
Satiny blooms in apricot, cream, lemon or white, pink and violet. Sow late as a hardy annual or grow as a half-hardy.
30 × 25cm/1ft × 10in

Nemesia fruticans
This little perennial, though not fully hardy, will self-seed and return next year. 10 × 15cm/ 8 × 6in

Nicotiana **(Tobacco flower)**
Indispensable, perfumed flowers of white, lime-green, crimson or dusky pink though some forms will not open their blossoms fully in daylight. Good in part-shade. The taller varieties have more grace.
45cm–1m × 45cm/1½–3ft × 1½ft

Petunia ❍
Single or double flowers in an extensive colour range, including many lurid bi-colors. Grown as a half-hardy annual, will bloom all summer till frosts. Must have full sun and are very resistant to drought. 22 × 15cm/9 × 6in

Verbena ❍
Edging plants which have a long flowering season, and are weather-resistant. Purple, lavender, red, pink or white flowers; *V. venosa* has rosy-purple flowers and produces tubers which can be lifted and stored. 45 × 30cm/1½ × 1ft

EASY HARDY ANNUALS

The plants on these pages are virtually foolproof to grow from seed. Moreover their variety makes them highly adaptable, some suited to fill a summer border in a new garden, others to occupy gaps after a death or before permanent plants have grown to their allotted span. Some will also act as charming edging plants.

***Echium* (*E. vulgare*)** ❍
Blue (also rose, mauve or white), long-flowering, easy, and bushy plants for edges or the rock garden. The form shown is called 'Blue Bedder'. 30cm/1ft H and W

Eschscholzia ❍
The California poppy has showy single or double flowers of red, mauve, pink, orange, yellow and cream with a long season. Good for poor, dry soils. 15–30 × 15cm/6in–1ft × 6in

Godetia
There are many varieties with single or double flowers in white, salmon, lilac, pink or carmine. Hardy annuals which are best in full sun but do quite well in part-shade. 30–60cm × 15–30cm/1–2ft × 6in–1ft

***Nigella damascena* (Love-in-a-mist)** ❍
Beautiful, easy annual with feathery foliage and white, rose, dark blue or pale blue flowers (this is the finest cultivar, called 'Miss Jekyll'), followed by handsome seed pods. 37 × 15cm/1ft 3in × 6in

CONSIDER ALSO:
Iberis umbellata (Candytuft) p.34
Nasturtium p.117

***Papaver somniferum* (Peony-flowered poppy)** ❍
An annual which can be single or double flowered and in a range of variable shades from pink to purple. Its glamorous flowers in summer are followed by showy seed heads. 1m × 30cm/3 × 1ft

Linum grandiflorum rubrum ❍
Most graceful, easy-to-grow plant bearing silky, crimson flowers with a dark eye. There is also a white variety. Mass in groups. 30 × 20cm/1ft × 8in

Planting a Border

Planting a border or a bed is one of the great pleasures. You are creating a picture out of a collection of plants and the possibilities are infinite. Lacy foliage against bold leaves, harmonies or contrasts of colour will make their own collective impact. Organized variety is what you seek. And if you choose carefully, a border can be stunning as well as easy to tend.

Labour-saving Perennials

One criticism levelled at the mixed border is that it involves its owner in hard work to make it prosper. This need not be true. A mixed border is easy to maintain so long as its inmates are carefully selected with this aim in mind. Plan it along the lines suggested on page 8, and when you come to choose hardy perennials, pick them from the following list. All the plants in this section have been chosen not only for their beauty but also for their labour-saving qualities. You won't need to stake them or lift and divide them regularly to keep them flourishing. If you give them the conditions they need, and mulch as required, they will thrive undisturbed in the same position for many years, and there are some which insist on being left alone for ever.

***Agapanthus* 'Headbourne Hybrids'** ❍
Handsome, relatively hardy clump-forming plants bearing large heads of deep or pale blue tubular flowers in mid-late summer. 75cm/2½ft H and W

***Aruncus dioicus* 'Kneiffii'** ◐
Mound-forming, cut-leafed foliage plant with creamy plumes of starry flowers in mid-summer. Part-shade and good, moist soil. 1m × 60cm/3 × 2ft

***Aquilegia* 'Snow Queen'**
White spurred flowers for early summer (for several months if dead-headed). Big colour range among other border hybrids. Short-lived perennials, best in light soil and longest flowering in part-shade. 60 × 45cm/2 × 1½ft

Astilbe ◐
Needs good, moist soil and part shade. There are many hybrids flowering in summer with a colour range through ruby, scarlet, pink and white. 'Erica', illustrated here, is 1m/3ft H and W.

Astrantia major
Easy, clump-forming plant in sun or shade with pin-cushion flowers surrounded by bracts. 60 × 45cm/2 × 1½ft. *A. maxima* is slightly more compact and has pinkish flowers with rosy bracts. Both flower for a long period in summer.

Aster × frikartii ❍
The easiest and one of the prettiest asters with lavender-blue flowers from midsummer until autumn. 75 × 45cm/2½ × 1½ft

***Centaurea hypoleuca* 'John Coutts'** ❍
Pink cornflowers throughout the summer above greyish leaves. Spreading plant which needs good drainage. 60 × 45cm/2 × 1½ft

Geranium psilostemon (syn. *armenum*) ❍
This bushy geranium has dark-eyed and very showy magenta flowers in summer. Leaves colour hotly in autumn. A light self-seeder in sun. Up to 1m/3ft H and W. See also the geraniums on pages 105, 173 and 174.

***Geranium* 'Johnson's Blue'**
A most accommodating clump-forming perennial with intense violet-blue flowers in summer over a mound of ground-covering foliage.
30 × 60cm/1 × 2ft

***Dicentra spectabilis* (Bleeding heart)** ◐
Beautiful, spring-border plant with heart-shaped rose-pink flowers. Most reliable in moist but well-drained soil and part-shade. There is a lovely white variety called 'Alba' which requires the same conditions. 60 × 45cm/2 × 1½ft

***Euphorbia griffithii* 'Fireglow'** ❍
This spurge is a fine cultivar with brick-red flower heads in early summer and strong, bushy spreading growth. 75 × 45cm/2½ × 1½ft. Other easy border candidates include *E. polychroma* (p. 60) and *E. characias ssp. wulfenii* (p. 55).

***Hemerocallis* 'Pink Damask' (Day lily)**
A reliable border plant producing a prolonged succession of summer flowers and handsome rushy leaves. Adaptable and easy. Innumerable cream, yellow, mahogany-red and pink cultivars exist ranging 60cm–1m × 60cm/2–3ft × 2ft.

Iris sibirica ❍
Arguably the easiest and best iris species for the border. Cultivars of white, blue, plum or violet obtainable. Moist soil preferred. The photograph shows 'Snow Bounty'. All flower in high summer. 1m × 60cm/3 × 2ft

Lilium regale
The easy and fragrant regal lily which is lime-tolerant. It needs planting deeply as it is stem-rooting. Summer-flowering. The form 'Album' differs only in that it is fully white rather than having a purple-flush on the outside of the flowers. Up to 1.2m × 30cm/4 × 1ft

Mertensia virginica ◐
A beautiful, spring-flowering, spreading plant for a cool soil and part-shade. Greyish leaves die down early. 45cm/1½ft H and W

Lychnis chalcedonica **(Maltese cross)** ❍
A true scarlet-flowered plant which needs light soil to thrive. It flowers in high summer. There are few other border plants of this colour. 1m × 45cm/3 × 1½ft

Peonies ❍
Essential border plants. Although their burst of flowers in early summer is short-lived, their foliage persists attractively. Of the different groups and many cultivars, the photograph shows *Paeonia lactiflora* 'Bowl of Beauty' 1m/3ft H and W. Never disturb peonies.

Polemonium reptans **'Lambrook Mauve'** ❍
A low-growing form of Jacob's ladder with attractive deep green foliage and clusters of lilac flowers en masse in early summer. 60cm/2ft H and W

***Rudbeckia fulgida* 'Goldsturm'** ❍
A vigorous cultivar, dwarfer than most which flowers from summer till autumn, producing a prolific display of golden, black-centred daisies. 75 × 45cm/2½ × 1½ft

Salvia* × *superba ❍
A robust, long-flowering plant with violet-purple spikes in summer. 1m × 45cm/3 × 1½ft. 'East Friesland' is a shorter cultivar at 45 cm/1½ft. 'May Night', illustrated here also 45cm/1½ft, begins to flower slightly earlier.

Sisyrinchium striatum E: ❍
Iris-like leaves and pale yellow spires of flowers in early summer. Good contrast to a horizontal-leafed neighbour. 60 × 22.5cm/2ft × 9in

***Sedum* 'Autumn Joy'** ❍
A most reliable, robust plant with succulent leaves and flat heads of russet flowers in autumn. 45cm/1½ft H and W

Sidalcea ❍
Spikes of mallow-like flowers of pink or red over a long season in summer. Leave undisturbed as long as possible. 75cm–1m × 45cm/2½–3ft × 1½ft depending on cultivar.

CONSIDER ALSO:

Anemone × *hybrida* p.144
Artemisia 'Lambrook Silver' p.68
Bergenia p.52
Brunnera macrophylla p.92
Epimedium p.104
Helleborus orientalis p.137
Hosta p.61
Kniphofia p.55
Nepeta × *faassenii* p.69
Tradescantia p.145

BORDER PERENNIALS

The plants on these pages demand a little more attention than those on the previous list.

***Alstroemeria* 'Ligtu hybrids'** ❍
Gorgeous summer flower–carmine to cream to salmon. Spreading where happy but can be hard to establish. Plant container-grown subjects and never disturb. Give rich soil and twiggy support to the taller cultivars. 30cm–1m × 60cm/1–3 × 2ft

***Anchusa azurea* 'Loddon Royalist'** ❍
One of the most intensely blue border perennials with sprays of small flowers in early summer and coarse hairy leaves. Stake 1.2m × 60cm/4 × 2ft

Campanula lactiflora
White, pink and lavender cultivars obtainable, and a rich blue called 'Prichard's Variety', which flower in summer, often until autumn. For moist, rich soil. Stake tall plants and do not disturb. 1.4m × 75cm/4 × 2½ft

Dendranthema (syn. *Chrysanthemum*) **'Ruby Mound'** ❍
A mass of glowing red flowers light the garden in autumn. 1.2m × 45cm/4 × 1½ft. Most chrysanthemums benefit from regular division and twiggy support.

Dierama pulcherrimum **(Angel's fishing-rod; Wandflower)** ❍
This graceful plant prefers light neutral to acid soil. Pink, rose or maroon bells in late summer over rushy leaves. Not fully hardy. 1m × 45cm/3 × 1½ft

Delphinium ❍
There are many named cultivars or, grown from seed, the Pacific Giant series in pink, white or pale to darkest blue, but these may dwindle after a few years. 1.2–1.8m × 60cm–1m/4–6ft × 2–3ft. 'Belladonna' varieties are shorter. Rich, moist soil and staking needed.

Eremurus bungei ❍
One of the magnificent fox-tail lilies, whose crowns and shoots are frost-tender and need protection before they emerge in spring. Avoid disturbance after planting as the roots are brittle. 1.5m × 45cm/5 × 1½ft

Helenium ❍
The most useful cultivars are those that flower from late summer through the autumn, such as the crimson-bronze 'Bruno' or the bronze-red 'Moorheim Beauty' illustrated here. Stake these taller varieties if they are in windy positions. 1m × 45cm/2 × 1½ft

Kirengeshoma palmata ◐ ●
A beautiful pale yellow, autumn-flowering, Japanese plant for shade and moist, leafy soil where it can spread. Good companion to shade-loving shrubs. 75 × 60cm/2½ × 2ft

Meconopsis betonicifolia LH: ◐
The Himalayan poppy has sky-blue poppy flowers in summer and hairy, glaucous leaves. Only perennial if plants are stopped from flowering in their first year: 1m × 4cm/3 × 1½ft. *M.* × *sheldonii* is a deeper blue. All need cool, leafy soil and part shade.

Lupinus hybrid **(Lupin)** ❍
Peppery-scented pea-flowers in summer. It is sometimes prone to mildew. 1m × 60cm/3 × 2ft

***Monarda* 'Croftway Pink'** ❍
A pretty cultivar of bergamot, a showy plant with flowers of red, pink, violet or white in summer to autumn. Regular division is beneficial. For moist but well-drained soil. 1m × 60cm/3 × 2ft

***Papaver orientale* 'Charming'** ❍
A pale-flowered form of the oriental poppy, all of which have showy flowers of pink, red, orange or white in early summer, often with a black base to the petals. Stake and cut down the untidy foliage after flowering. Don't disturb. 1m × 75cm/3 × 2ft

***Phlox paniculata* 'Little Lovely'** ◐
A shorter-growing example of the scented phlox, which has late summer flowers of lavender, purple, pink, red, salmon, or white. Needs moist soil and prefers part-shade. Division every three years necessary. Often menaced by eelworm. 60cm–1m × 60cm/ 2–3ft × 2ft

TENDER PERENNIALS FOR SHELTERED POSITIONS

In cold regions, all the following plants will need lifting or protection during the winter.

Dahlia merckii ❍
A graceful variety that is very different from the showy fat-flowered cultivars grown in most borders. It blooms from summer until autumn. The tubers may need lifting for the winter, or give them a thick winter-covering in a sheltered place if left in the ground. 1m/3ft H and W

***Lobelia* 'Dark Crusader'** ❍
Rich red velvety flowers in late summer distinguish this tender perennial, which enjoys moist soil. In cold regions the crowns will need covering for winter protection. 1m × 30cm/3 × 1ft

Felicia amelloides ❍
The brilliant blue yellow-eyed kingfisher daisy will make a sparkling small bush all summer to autumn, if it can be lifted and brought through the winter. 45cm/1½ft H and W

Salvia buchananii ❍
One of the sages with magenta lipped, velvety flowers in summer and glossy dark green leaves. It will need protection under glass in winter. If it is dead-headed, it will produce flowers over a longer period. 60cm/2ft H and W

Salvia patens ❍
Rich azure flowers are produced throughout the summer on this tuberous perennial which has softly hairy leaves. Lift the tubers before winter or give them frost protection in the ground. 60cm/2ft H and W

Edge-breakers

No bed or border ever looks luxuriant or even comfortable if it stops short of its edge. The plants seem self-conscious, as though they are only perching there but have not taken root and settled in. This stiff appearance can be avoided if you plant along the edge the kind of spreading subjects which will spill over the boundary. The most useful plants are evergreen, but there are also many herbaceous candidates with lush, bold leaves and arching stems which will be effective from spring to autumn. For the shrub border, the most valuable are either the less rampant prostrate evergreen shrubs or else those under 1m/3ft with a rounded habit which will sit like hummocks at and over the edge. To simplify mowing the adjacent lawn lay a line of paving (mowing-stones) at the edge of the bed below the level of the grass.

Artemisia canescens Semi-E: ❍
A splendid bushy perennial with very finely cut leaves curling like silver wire. It will make good ground cover. 45cm/1½ft H and W

Campanula alliariifolia
Clump-forming perennial with long, heart-shaped, grey-green leaves and stems of ivory flowers for many weeks in summer and intermittently in autumn. 45cm/1½ft H and W

***Dianthus* 'Mrs Sinkins'** ❍
One of the favourite old pinks, with a messily-presented flower as it often bursts its calyx, yet so heavily scented that it is still grown. 15 × 25cm/6 × 10in

***Hakonechloa macra* 'Alboaurea'** ❍
A golden Japanese grass with some green and fawn variegation. Yellowish inflorescence in late summer. A dazzling low edger. 45cm/1½ft H and W

***Geranium cinereum* 'Ballerina'** ❍
Appealing rosetted perennial with dusky pink, dark-eyed and dark-veined flowers in early summer onwards for a long period. 10 × 30cm/4in × 1ft

CONSIDER ALSO:

Anthemis cupaniana p.214
Carex comans p.86
Geranium p.105
Helictotrichon sempervirens p.86
Hemerocallis p.82
Nepeta × faassenii p.69
Stachys byzantina p.69
Stipa gigantea p.87

Liriope muscari E: ❍
Valuable, labour-saving plant with rushy evergreen leaves and spikes of small violet flowers over a long period late in the year. 30cm/1ft H and W

***Veronica austriaca* ssp. *teucrium* 'Corfu Form'**
A good edge-breaker for a low wall or a bank where its sprays of intensely blue small flowers will mass the plant in early summer. 20 × 30cm/10 × 1ft

Ferns E: ◐
The evergreen *Polystichum setiferum* 'Divisilobum' is illustrated here with its lacy, finely divided fronds, one of the best of the ground spraying ferns. Needs well-drained soil. 50 × 60cm/1ft 8in × 2ft. The deciduous *Athyrium* (p. 53) and evergreen hart's tongue fern (p. 110) are also first choices.

***Geranium clarkei* 'Kashmir White'**
A graceful perennial with white mauve-veined drooping flowers in summer held over a mound of finely cut leaves which make spreading ground-cover. 30 × 45cm/1 × 1½ft

***Geranium macrorrhizum* 'Bevan's Variety'**
A groundcover plant with aromatic leaves that colour richly in autumn and magenta flowers in spring to early summer. Other forms have white or lilac flowers. It will self-seed. 30cm/1ft H and W

***Hosta* 'Frances Williams'** ◐
A very handsome cultivar making a mound of ribbed leaves which are greyish-green with yellow edges, fading with age. It has lilac flowers in summer. 75cm/2½ft H and W

***Saxifraga* × *urbium* (London pride)** E: ❍ ◐ ●
This neat accommodating plant is happy wherever it is grown. Its prostrate leaf rosettes will spread to form a neat edging over paving. It has pale or deep pink sprays of starry flowers in late spring/early summer. There is also a variegated form. 25cm/10in × indefinite spread

CONSIDER ALSO:

Alchemilla mollis p.52
Bergenia p.52
Campanula 'Birch Hybrid' p.100
Helleborus foetidus p.113
H. orientalis p.137
Hosta in variety
Tellima grandiflora p.105

Heuchera (Alum root) E: ◐
Virtually evergreen leaves surmounted by dainty flowers of white, cream, pink or shades of red in early summer. The photograph shows *H.* 'Rachel'.
45 × 30cm/1½ × 1ft

***Philadelphus* 'Manteau d'Hermine'**
A compact domed mock orange, covered with scented white double flowers in early to midsummer. It will make a pouffe at the front of a shrub or mixed border. 1 × 1.5m/3 × 5ft

Ballota pseudodictamnus E: ❍
A sub-shrub with soft and hairy grey-green rounded leaves and whorls of tiny pink flowers and green calyces. It is not fully hardy and needs a well-drained soil. 60cm × 1m/2 × 3ft

CONSIDER ALSO:

Artemisia 'Powis Castle' p.88
Helianthemum p.96
Lavender p.207
Ruta graveolens p.71

***Hebe* 'Pewter Dome'** E: ❍
There are a number of valuable evergreen hebes for this position. This one makes a spreading, grey, small-leafed mound with white flower-spikes in summer. 75cm × 1m/2½ × 3ft. See also *H. rakaiensis* (syn. *subalpina*) on page 107.

***Picea pungens glauca* 'Procumbens'** E
Stunningly blue, prostrate spruce which is suited to the front of a conifer- or rock-border. Its stiffness makes it an alien in the conventional setting of the mixed, deciduous border. 15cm × 1m/6in × 3ft

Penstemon glaber Semi-E: ❍
A wonderful sub-shrub for ground-cover, with blue and pink flowerbells for a long period in summer. It is reasonably hardy in a sheltered position, but the old flowering stems should not be cut back until spring. 40 × 60cm/1ft 4in × 2ft

Salvia lavandulifolia E: ❍
A bushy sage with slender greyish-green leaves and sprays of mauve flowers that make a great show in summer. It needs well-drained soil as it is not fully hardy. 75cm/2½ft H and W

***Santolina rosmarinifolia ssp. rosmarinifolia* (Green cotton lavender)** E: ❍
Rich green leaves and flat flower-heads in summer. Will spread out, but a number grouped together will form a fuller mound. 45cm/1½ft H and W

Daphne pontica E ◐ ●
This shrub makes an increasingly spreading dome of neat evergreen foliage with very scented lime-yellow flowers in spring. 1 × 1.2m/3 × 4ft

Consider also the smaller, bushy hydrangeas such as *H.* 'Preziosa'; also *Skimmia japonica* p.127 and *Viburnum davidii* p.109.

Rhododendron: Azalea E: LH: ◐
The most suitable azaleas for edging positions are the spring-flowering, evergreen varieties which form spreading bushes of 60cm–1.2m/2–4ft. There is a colour range of white, pink, red, orange, lavender and violet. 'Hinomayo' shown here, is a Japanese hybrid, belonging to the Kurume group, an old and reliable variety massed with clear pink flowers in late spring. 60cm × 1m/2 × 3ft

Rhododendron E: LH: ◐
Of the thousands of this genus under cultivation, the most useful in a front-of-border position are those which have a neat, mounded habit. Of these, *R. williamsianum* (above) is an exquisite species with heart-shaped leaves and pale pink or white bell flowers in spring. 60cm × 1.2m/2 × 4ft

Back-of-border Shrubs

The back of a border is a position best reserved for certain kinds of plants. First, for the tallest, most corpulent shrubs which will act as a visual stop and a background to the plants in front. Second, for frost-tender or doubtfully hardy plants which will be safer if protected by a wall or fence. Third, for shrubs which bloom at a cold season of the year and whose blossoms will be less vulnerable here to bad weather. Fourth, for the kind of tall or medium-size old favourites like lilacs or buddlejas, with beautiful flowers but undistinguished foliage or habit. Fifth, for climbers or semi-scandent shrubs which need either the support of a wall or a large plant to entwine. Lastly, a high proportion of evergreens is essential here, especially if the border is much in view from the house during winter; for this group of plants, see especially pages 48–51 and the large evergreens on pages 62–7.

Abutilon* × *suntense ❍
A beautiful hybrid abutilon which is only frost hardy. It bears in profusion rich mauve saucer-flowers in early summer and has grey-green foliage. 3m × 1.8m/10 × 6ft

Abutilon vitifolium ❍
Equally beautiful with greyish foliage and either soft lavender (or white in the form 'Album') flowers in early summer. Not fully hardy. 3 × 1.8m/10 × 6ft

Buddleja crispa ❍
A soft felted grey foliaged shrub with lilac orange-throated flowers for a long period in summer to autumn. Not fully hardy. 2.4m/8ft H and W

Callistemon rigidus E: O
An Australian shrub with rich red-stamened bottlebrush flowers in early summer. In cold-winter areas it needs to be trained on a wall for greater shelter where it may reach 3m/10ft.

***Ceanothus* 'Trewithen Blue'** E or semi-E: ❍
One of the more tender ceanothus with large panicles of rich blue flowers in early summer. Vigorous to 6m/20ft H and W

***Clianthus puniceus* (Lobster claw plant)** Semi-E: ❍
Gorgeous tender wall-shrub with ferny foliage and coral (or white) pendent flowers in summer. Best trained on a wire-mesh support. Up to 3m/10ft

CONSIDER ALSO:

Carpenteria californica p.50
Ceanothus in variety p.50
Cistus in variety p.122
Choisya ternata p.48
Cytisus battandieri p.72
Fremontodendron 'Californian Glory' p.222
Solanum crispum 'Glasnevin' p.229

***Escallonia* 'Iveyi'** E: ❍
A vigorous, bushy evergreen with shining leaves and showy panicles of small white flowers from summer to autumn. Not fully hardy. 4 × 3m/ 13 × 10ft

Hoheria lyallii ❍
A large grey-green leafed shrub or small tree which will need pruning on wall space. An avalanche of fragrant small white flowers in summer. 4 × 3m/13 × 10ft

Itea ilicifolia E: ❍
An evergreen shrub with holly-like leaves and long ice-green fragrant catkin inflorescences in summer to 30cm/1ft or more. Not fully hardy. 3m/10ft H and W

***Buddleja davidii* (Butterfly bush)** ❍
A shrub with a leggy habit and long scented panicles in summer of lavender, white, purple-red or dark purple. The form shown is 'Dartmoor' presenting its flowers in multiple plumes. 3 × 2.1m/10 × 7ft

Cotoneaster horizontalis
This will lean its way up a wall where it is notable for its attractive fish-bone habit. Insignificant white flowers in spring followed by showy red berries in autumn. A form with cream-variegated leaves is obtainable. Up to 4m/13ft on a wall.

***Chaenomeles* × *superba* 'Pink Lady' (Japonica)**
A spring-blooming shrub which does well if it is trained as a wall-specimen. It should be pruned after flowering, reducing side shoots to 2 or 3 buds. To 1.8m/6ft on a wall.

Paeonia delavayi* var. *ludlowii ❍
The largest tree peony with elegantly cut foliage and glowing golden bowls of flowers in early summer. Shield shoots in early spring from morning sun and frost. 2.4m/8ft H and W

***Syringa* 'Missumo' (Lilac)** ❍
There are many cultivars of this familiar large shrub, with single or double scented flowers of pink, lilac-blue, purple, white or lemon in early summer. 5m/16ft H and W

***Philadelphus* 'Belle Etoile' (Mock orange)** ❍
One of the loveliest scented philadelphus with a dark staining at the base of its petals. It flowers in summer. 2.1m/7ft H and W

***Syringa* × *josiflexa* 'Bellicent'** ❍
A Canadian hybrid lilac with large plumes of graceful pendent pink flowers in early summer. It is very fragrant. 4 × 5m/13 × 16ft

Perennials for Pool Borders or Moist Sites

There are many plants which actually need conditions that are permanently moist in order to thrive. These are a gardener's first choice when it comes to planting a bog garden or the margins of a pool or a stream. They are a varied and handsome lot. Some of these plants have bold architectural leaves and are equally attractive whether in or out of flower. Others, such as those from the primula family, include some of the most beautiful flowers one can grow. If you are making a pool border, it is a good idea to choose a proportion which spray over the edges of the pool and form green waterfalls themselves. This ensures they will conceal the ugly join between water and earth (or liner).

***Caltha palustris* 'Flore Pleno'** ❍
A double form of the marsh marigold which forms bold clumps of gold in spring above dark green leaves. It is not quite as spreading as the single form. 30cm/1ft H and W

***Darmera peltata* (Umbrella plant)**
Handsome, spreading foliage plant for moist soil round larger pools. Pink sprays of flowers in spring followed by large round leaves, usually colouring well in autumn. Good companion for grassy-leafed plants. 1m × 60cm/ 3 × 2ft

Gunnera manicata
Giant-leafed waterside subject for large areas. Its inflorescences appear in early summer. Establish in spring and cover crowns in winter with its dead leaves as frost-protection. It is not fully hardy. 3m/10ft H and W

Iris ensata (syn. *kaempferi*)
LH
The Japanese iris has most beautiful velvety flowers in midsummer of purple, blue, mauve, red or white. It can be tricky as it needs plenty of water when growing but drier conditions in winter.
1m × 30cm/3 × 1ft

***Iris pseudacorus* 'Bastardii'**
The variegated form of the wild yellow flag, which produces golden flowers in early summer. It is less invasive than the self-seeding plain green form which is only suited to larger areas.
1.2m × 30cm/4 × 1ft

***Iris versicolor* 'Kermesina'**
A lovely North American with plum-purple flowers veined and marked with gold in early summer. It will grow in wet mud, or very shallow water or in a moist border. 75 × 30cm/2½ × 1ft

Ligularia przewalskii
Spires of golden flowers rise in mid to late summer above mounds of bold jagged leaves. It is a vigorous grower in rich, moist soil where it will make a statuesque clump. 1.5 × 1m/5 × 3ft

***Lysichiton americanus* (Skunk cabbage)**
This has large yellow spathes in spring followed by big cabbage-like leaves of bright green. It will grow in the margins of a pool or in a moist or wet soil.
1.2 × 1m/4 × 3ft

***Mimulus* 'Orange Glow'**
There are many hybrids of the familiar monkey flower, forming spreading carpets of colour with a long flowering-season. They are mostly short-lived perennials and not fully hardy. 20cm/8in H and W

Lysichiton camtschatcensis
This lysichiton is a smaller version from the Orient with white spathes in spring. Apart from its colour and size, it is similar to its larger relative and has the same cultural needs. 75 × 60cm/2½ × 2ft

***Osmunda regalis* (Royal fern)** LH
Splendid deciduous, autumn-colouring fern for moist, acid soil with erect fronds up to 1.8m/6ft but usually less. Prefers shade but will usually stand full sun in soil full of humus. Usually 1.2m × 45cm/ 4 × 1½ft

***Primula denticulata* (Drumstick primula)**
A tough spring-flowering primula with round flowerheads of mauve or white. 30cm/1ft H and W

***Primula florindae* (Himalayan cowslip)**
A large imposing primula with clusters of pendent yellow flowers in later summer. There is also a form with flowers of a dusky red. 1m × 45cm/3 × 1½ft

Primula pulverulenta
An excellent candelabra primula with tiers of magenta blossoms in early summer and mealy white stems. The 'Bartley' form has buff or pink flowers. 45 × 30cm/1½ × 1ft

***Primula* 'Valley Red' ● ◐**
A fine selected form of candelabra primula which is a sound perennial and looks dramatic when planted in mass. Its richly coloured tiers of flowers bloom in early summer. 30cm/1ft H and W

Primula vialii
A beautiful but short-lived species with parti-coloured pokers of unopened red flowers at the top and open lilac at the bottom in summer. 30 × 20cm/1ft × 8in

***Rheum palmatum* (Ornamental rhubarb)**
A stunning foliage plant grown chiefly for its bold deeply lobed foliage. In early summer, tall plumes of white flowers, or red in the form 'Atrosanguineum', rise above the leaves. 1.8 × 1m/6 × 3ft

Sinacalia tangutica (syn. Senecio tanguticus)
A handsome perennial with large conical heads of small golden daisy flowers in late summer to autumn over jagged deeply cut foliage. A spreader even in clay soil. 1.5m × 60cm/ 5 × 2ft

***Trollius chinensis* 'Golden Queen'**
A beautiful marginal plant with orange globular flowers in early summer. There are many good globe flowers including forms with pale creamy blooms.
60 × 30cm/2 × 1ft

***Zantedeschia aethiopica* 'Crowborough'** ❍
Fairly hardy arum lily flowering for a long season, summer to autumn. A plant for the moist border, but it will also grow in shallow water. In either case, its tubers should be protected from frost. 60cm/2ft H and W

CONSIDER ALSO:

Astilbe in variety p.161
Filipendula rubra p.21
Gentiana asclepiadea p.110
Hosta in variety
Lysimachia punctata p.23
Persicaria bistorta 'Superba' p.105
Rodgersia in variety p.105
Telekia speciosa p.24

Ornamental Herbs

Give herbs an area to themselves because many self-sow furiously. But if space is limited, some are ornamental enough to merit a place in the border. All self-sowers will need sharp watching; seed-heads should be removed and seedlings which develop outside the allotted territory should be dug up. Plant herbs in sun unless otherwise stated.

Angelica (*Angelica archangelica*)
Decorative in leaf and creamy flower. Perennial if stopped from flowering. Stems can be crystallized. Self-sowing. 1.4m × 60cm/ 5 × 2ft

Bay (*Laurus nobilis*) E
A dark, aromatic-leafed evergreen shrub which lends itself to topiary. Needs shelter in a harsh winter as it is not fully hardy. Height according to pruning.

Borage (*Borago officinalis*)
An annual with pretty, stamened, blue flowers above coarse, hairy leaves. Invasively self-sowing. 40 × 22cm/ 1ft 4in × 9in

Chervil (*Anthriscus cerefolium*)
A self-sowing annual with dainty, feathery leaves which will persist through the winter if autumn sown. Useful for egg dishes. 30 × 22cm/1ft × 9in

Chives (*Allium schoenoprasum*)
Useful edging plant with pink-purple flowers. The giant variety, *A.s. sibiricum,* is more decorative. Cut leaves from base to ensure a succession of shoots. 25 × 22cm/ 10 × 9in

Fennel (*Foeniculum vulgare*)
Feathery, green foliage but the bronze variety is more beautiful. Cut off golden flowerheads (unless seeds are for kitchen use) to prevent self-sowing and attain bushier plants. 1.2 × 1m/4 × 3ft

Hyssop (*Hyssopus officinalis*) E
Can be used in stews and salads but now grown chiefly as a useful evergreen sub-shrub with rich blue (or pink) flowers. 45cm/1½ft H and W

Marigold (*Calendula officinalis*)
An annual with a tradition as a border plant. Its orange-yellow petals can be used in salads. Invasively self-sowing. 45 × 30cm/1½ × 1ft

Lovage (*Levisticum officinale*)
A shapely plant with purple stems and glossy leaves which give a celery tang to stews. The stems can be crystallized when young and the seeds are sometimes used in baking. 1.2 × 1m/4 × 3ft

Marjoram
The variety *Origanum vulgare* 'Aureum' has golden leaves and dusty pink flowers.
30 × 45cm/1 × 1½ft

Mints can be decorative but their running rootstock can be very invasive if they are planted in a bed or border. It is more convenient if they are confined to a large pot or self-contained corner. There are two mints with especially pretty foliage.

***Mentha* × *gentilis* 'Variegata' (Ginger mint)** ◐ (above)
Decorative gold and green mint which is also very invasive. Best grown in a container to curb its running tendencies. The leaf-tips are sometimes used in salads. 60cm/2ft × indefinite spread

***Mentha suaveolens* 'Variegata' (Variegated apple mint)** ◐
A variegated cream and grey-green mint which is grown for its attractive summer foliage. 45 × 60cm/1½ × 2ft

Winter savory (*Satureja montana*) E
An evergreen sub-shrub with small mauve flowers. 30cm/1ft H and W

You can supplement this list with violas, pansies and nasturtiums whose flowers are edible. All these are possible front-of-border candidates. And don't forget rosemary (p.115), sage (p.115), golden balm (p.61) and thyme, of which the lemon, the caraway and the common thyme (*T. vulgaris*) are the best cooking varieties.

Parsley (*Petroselinum crispum*)
An excellent edging plant or can be used in front-of-border groups in sun or shade. Biennial but sow annually for succession. 15cm/6in H and W

Trees, Hedges and Backgrounds

These are usually the dominant fundamentals in an area, partly because of their size. They are important for different reasons. Trees give height and shade to a garden, whereas hedges define its shape. Climbers are glamorous vertical furnishings, and large background features like pergolas or topiary give a garden a powerful individuality. The right choice and use of any of these plants or plant features is crucial because of their size and dominance.

Trees, Hedges and Backgrounds

Dominant plant features of this type should not usually be afterthoughts. They are the first fundamentals to which you add the smaller furnishings like beds and borders. If you are re-designing your whole garden or working on a blank canvas, here is your starting-point. If you simply want to add a hedge or a main feature to an existing garden, then be prepared for the possibility that it may dictate further changes.

The fact is that, even though such features may form backgrounds to other plants in the garden, they are part of its actual structure and therefore a key element in its design.

This is especially true of hedges. These are just as important as the partitions of a house, defining not only a room's extent, but its shape as well. They have a number of additional purposes to fulfil too. They give privacy, they screen unwanted views, they protect against intruders, and they give wind shelter also. They are actually far more effective against wind than solid walls, for they filter its force instead of blocking it and thereby causing undue turbulence and eddying.

The type of hedge you choose is an important decision. The possibilities are enormous, yet your requirements may narrow this array to a handful. You must decide whether you want it to be evergreen or deciduous; to flower, fruit or berry; to back a border, front a garden, or define a path. Do you want extreme formality or the irregularity of free growth? Would you like the type of hedge which is suited to incorporating 'windows' and 'doorways'? Do you want a circular or curving hedge? How often are you prepared to clip it and how much room do you have? On a more practical note, how much are you prepared to pay, for different varieties can vary greatly in price.

Whatever your choice, remember that it is likely to become a permanent feature in the garden; you will live with it for a long time.

A newly clipped hedge of copper beech.

Hedges: Preparation Planting and Aftercare

Planning is essential. The easiest way of choosing the site for a hedge is to test out its line in advance with string stretched along pegs. (Most hedges follow a straight line, but if you want a curved or circular hedge, use a centrally placed batten and attach to it a string lead which can be swivelled in an arc.) Then, visualize how the fully-grown hedge will look in this position; or, alternatively, take a photograph of the area and draw in the hedge on the print. When planning the site, take into account any eyesores that should be screened. Consider, too, where you need your openings and, if there is to be more than one aperture, are they lined up if necessary? Finally, make sure that you allow room for the hedge's thickness; as much as 1m/3ft from the nearest plants in a border, and not less than 60cm/2ft distance from a path.

Calculating the Number of Plants

This estimate will depend on the intervals required between the plants. Remember that the first and last plants don't go in at the very end of a row, but at a distance of half the usual interval, to allow for their eventual spread. The number of plants will also vary (obviously) if you plant a double row (or even treble) of staggered plants with the purpose of making an extra-strong barrier.

Digging the Soil

When you have decided on the site, kill off all perennial weeds in the area with a weed-killer that does not poison the soil. Then, dig a trench along the line of string and pegs to a spade's depth and about 1m/3ft width for a single row of plants. (Increase this width to 1.5m/5ft if you will be planting a double row.) If the soil is seriously waterlogged, the soil must be dug to double the spade's depth and, without bringing the lower spit of subsoil to the upper spit, insert plastic drainage pipes and rubble. Otherwise, the hedge will simply perish. To give any hedge a good start, work old dung, compost or fertilizer into the trench but cover this with good topsoil so that the hedge's roots are not in direct contact with it.

Planting

You can plant deciduous hedges any time between autumn and spring so long as the soil isn't frozen or sticky with rain. Plant evergreens in early autumn or mid-late spring when the soil is warmer. In a cold or exposed spot, evergreens will also need some protection against icy, scourging winds, to prevent them suffering from wind-burn which can be fatal. In this case, erect in advance polythene sheeting (supported on stakes) on the wind-exposed side of the planting line.

To ensure you plant your hedge in an absolutely straight (or perfectly curved) line, make an indentation in the earth or nick out the soil to a spade's depth immediately below the taut string you have stretched on pegs. Keeping accurately to this indentation, plant each shrub to the depth of its original soil line, having spread out the roots on bare-rooted plants. Put the finest soil around the roots before filling in the rest of the hole with earth. Firm down the soil around each plant to prevent it suffering from wind-rock. Tall, thin plants may need to be tied to a stake and, in this case, the pole should be fixed stoutly in the planting hole in advance.

Watering and Mulching

The young hedge will have to be kept watered in dry weather, and this is especially important for evergreens which can die in a spring drought. Mulch the hedge also to conserve moisture.

Clipping

The most suitable pruning time/s for each variety of hedge are given in the description for each individual shrub. But as a general principle, those that need hard clipping in their early years to induce lush growth at the base can be cut back in the spring of the following year if they are spring planted, or 18 months after autumn planting. Otherwise, let the leader or growing shoot continue until the desired height is reached, but trim the side shoots regularly.

Always make sure that the base of the hedge is broader and bushier than the top. This produces a sloping effect which is called a batter. It allows light and air to reach the lower branches which encourages strong growth; it prevents gappiness at the base; it results in greater stability.

Hedges lend themselves also to a variety of decorative treatments. You can give them 'doors' and 'windows'; you can top them with topiary; you can trim them to form stilt hedges which look like slim, green boxes on poles.

Feeding

All trimmed hedges respond to being fed, for severe clipping makes demands on the shrubs. To keep them in peak condition, give them old manure or compost, bonemeal or liquid manure in the spring.

Evergreen Hedges

Tall, dense, evergreen hedges are virtually living walls and can be used as such. At all times of the year, they form barriers within a garden and redoubtable boundaries around it. Some of those listed below are far too big for small gardens, as they will outgrow their station on reaching maturity. Others, however, can be kept clipped into slimness and should be preferred where space is short. Some flower and fruit, others give a more self-effacing display but lend themselves to intricate trimming to provide doorways, windows and topiary shapes. Quick-growing varieties are more demanding, as they require clipping three or even four times a year. The slow hedges make you wait, but repay this disadvantage by needing only one annual clip. Varieties with very large leaves look best if they are hand-trimmed with secateurs to avoid mutilating their foliage, and in such cases, the length of hedge should be taken into account. A few varieties are toxic to stock and should not be grown where animals can reach the leaves.

Aucuba japonica E
Handsome hedge especially in the variegated form or berrying (female) clones. Tolerant of poor soil and shade. Large leaves need careful trimming with secateurs. Plant 1m/3ft apart.
2.4m/8ft

Berberis* × *stenophylla E
Vigorous, dark, dense hedge with an arching habit of growth. Its thorns help to keep out intruders. Gold flowers in early spring. Plant 45cm/1½ft apart. Clip after flowering.
2.4m/8ft

***Buxus sempervirens* 'Handsworthensis'** E **(Box)**
Makes a dark formal hedge up to 4m/13ft with aromatic leaves. Needs well-drained soil and is good on chalk. Plant 45cm/1½ft apart. Trim in early summer and again, if needed, in early autumn.

Chamaecyparis lawsoniana **(Lawson cypress)** E
Coniferous hedge which is good in wind and part-shade. There are many cultivars of different shades from blue to bright green to gold. Normal rate of growth is about 60cm/2ft a year, but 'Ellwoodii' (above), with grey-green foliage, steel blue in winter, is a much slower cultivar, reducing the need to clip. Plant about 1m/3ft apart.

× ***Cupressocyparis leylandii*** **(Leyland cypress)** E
Another coniferous hedge with phenomenally speedy growth needing at least three trims a year. It soon outgrows its station. Plant 1m/3ft apart.

Cotoneaster franchetii var. ***sternianus*** E
A beautiful hedge which can be kept slim, bearing white flowers in spring and coral berries. Sage-green leaves with a silver underside. Plant 45cm/1½ft apart. Trim after growth has finished. 2.4m/8ft

Cotoneaster lacteus
This cotoneaster is vigorous and fast-growing with long-lasting red berries that follow on from its small white flowers. It is tolerant of most soils. Plant 45cm/1½ft apart. 2.4m/8ft

× ***Cupressocyparis leylandii*** **'Castlewellan'** E
This popular golden form of Leyland cypress is sometimes called 'Galway Gold'. It does not grow quite so quickly as the green form.

Olearia macrodonta E
A reasonably hardy shrub with holly-like leaves, sage-green above and silvery beneath, and a profuse display of white daisy flowers in summer. Best on acid soil. Plant in spring 1m/3ft apart. Clip after flowering 2.1m/7ft

Pyracantha in variety (**Firethorn**) E
This tough shrub with its white flowers in spring followed by a display of berries makes a handsome hedge especially if yellow and red fruited varieties are mixed. 3m/10ft

Ilex (**Holly**) E
Many hollies make excellent hedges in sun or shade and on any soil. *Ilex* × *altaclarensis* 'Camelliifolia' is dark green and almost spineless. At the other extreme is *Ilex aquifolium* 'Ferox Argentea', (shown here) the silver hedgehog holly, with spines on the upperside as well as around its leaves. Margins and spines are creamy-white. Plant about 45–60cm/1½–2ft apart. Ultimate height around 8m/26ft if required.

Prunus laurocerasus (**Laurel**) E
This makes an attractive bright hedge with its glossy emerald foliage but can look ugly after clipping if its large leaves have been cut in two by the machine. Plant 1m/3ft apart. 3m/10ft

***Taxus baccata* (Yew)** E
A superb hedge which is tolerant of most soils except those that are waterlogged. It grows about 30cm/1ft a year and is clipped in late summer. Ideal for arches or topiary trimmings. Plant 60cm–1m/2–3ft apart. 5m/16ft

Tapestry hedges
Hedges can be made out of a variety of plants. The secret of a successful tapestry hedge is to combine plants whose habits and rates of growth are similar. The effect is particularly dramatic when the hedge design emphasises the different plants as here where gold and green conifers form a battlemented combination.

Thuja plicata E
The western red cedar is a fast-growing hedge needing two clips, but is suited to a narrow space as it can be kept slim. Plant 60cm/2ft apart. 3m/10ft or more. *T. occidentalis* is a slowish-growing conifer thriving in any well-drained soil with many cultivars of green or gold. Needs clipping only once a year.

This tapestry hedge combines deciduous as well as evergreen plants. The effect is wonderful but needs careful management to ensure that the stronger-growing inmates do not take over the weaker.

Formally Clipped Deciduous Hedges

A formally clipped deciduous hedge will form as effective a barrier or background when in leaf as any evergreen hedge, but in winter most varieties will be see-through. An exception to this is beech (*Fagus*) which retains its dead leaves, and also, to a lesser extent, hornbeam (*Carpinus*).

***Crataegus monogyna* (Hawthorn)**
Not for formal surroundings, but makes a good, cheap, clipped hedge in the country. Thorny, tough, tolerant of any soil and adaptable to topiary. White flowers in late spring and dark red fruit in autumn. Plant 30cm/1ft apart and trim in late autumn. 4m/13ft

***Carpinus betulus* (Hornbeam)**
A strong, dense hedge resembling beech, to which it is far superior on heavy, wet soils. It retains its withered donkey-brown leaves throughout the winter if clipped in late summer. Plant 45–60cm/1½–2ft apart. Up to 5m/16ft if necessary.

***Fagus sylvatica* (Beech)**
Probably the best formal, deciduous hedge and good on all well-drained soils. Its leaves turn russet in autumn and, if pruned in late summer, will remain throughout the winter. Good topiary subject. Plant 45–60cm/1½–2ft apart and don't trim the leaders until the desired height is reached.

***Prunus cerasifera* 'Pissardii' (or 'Nigra')**
A small tree which can be grown as a vigorous, bushy hedge. At its finest in spring when starred with pale pink flowers, but its foliage, first ruby then deepening to black-purple, is a useful contrast to a pale border near it. Unfortunately it needs clipping three times a year and needs careful siting for maximum convenience. Plant 75cm/2½ft apart. 3.5m/12ft

Flowering Hedges

Another category of hedge which can make an ornamental screen or division is the deciduous hedge formed of attractive flowering shrubs. Its effect is at the opposite extreme from the dark and severe architecture of most formal boundary or border hedges. Many of the varieties are allowed to grow fairly freely, or, if pruned, given only a slight trim rather than carved into a rectangular block. The tougher, larger varieties will make powerful windbreaks. The more floriferous and ornamental are better treated as garden features in their own right, perhaps, for example, bordering a grass walk where they serve to replace a border, being spreading, linear and colourful. Some are even sometimes used as boundary shrubs around a front garden but, being deciduous, provide inadequate cover in winter. But, wherever they are placed, nearly all these colour hedges need siting with care. The massed colours of some flowers can be overpowering and even offensive if placed near hot competition.

***Fuchsia* 'Riccartonii'**
This fuchsia is the hardiest of all varieties, making a beautiful informal hedge in sheltered gardens. Plant 45cm/1½ft apart and trim in early spring if necessary. 1.2m/4ft

***Chaenomeles* × *superba* 'Crimson and Gold' (Japonica)**
This spreading shrub makes a fine bright hedge in spring when it flowers, after which it can be clipped. Here it is grown against a railing which gives extra support. The form 'Rowallane' also makes a good hedge. Plant 60cm/2ft apart. 1.2m/4ft

***Hydrangea arborescens* 'Grandiflora' ◐**
A loose shrub which bears great domes of greenish-white flowers in summer through till autumn. It is inclined to loll and is best against support like a low wall. Plant 60cm–1m/2–3ft apart and trim in early spring. 1m/3ft

FLOWERING HEDGES

Certain groups of shrub roses make the most beautiful of all deciduous flowering hedges though they must be encouraged to become bushy at the base before developing. Cut them back hard in the spring following planting. Thereafter prune lightly, but remove weak or dead growth.

***Rosa* 'Roseraie de l'Haÿ'** ❍
One of the best examples from the Rugosa rose group. It bears very fragrant, velvety, purplish-crimson large flowers with golden stamens recurrently from early summer till autumn. Plant 1m/3ft apart. 1.8m/6ft. 'Scabrosa' with single magenta flowers and large hips is also suitable. 1.5m/5ft

***Rosa* 'Penelope'** ❍
This creamy-pink hybrid musk rose which is very scented makes a good healthy hedge. It flowers for a long period from early summer onwards. 1.8m/6ft

***Rosa* 'Queen Elizabeth'** ❍
This floribunda, or cluster-flowered, rose is a popular hedging choice. It blooms continuously and is strong and vigorous. 1.5m/5ft

Rosa mundi (*Rosa gallica versicolor*) ❍
An old French (Gallica) rose that has bright green foliage and very fragrant pink cerise-striped flowers. It makes a wonderful once-flowering low hedge. 1.2m/4ft

CONSIDER ALSO:
Rosa glauca p.91

***Viburnum opulus* 'Sterile' (Snowball bush)**
This forms a much more showy hedge with large white globular flowerheads in early summer. It is infertile, so no fruit follows. Its leaves colour well in autumn. 2.4m/8ft

***Viburnum opulus* (Guelder rose)**
This makes a pretty informal hedge for wilder areas with white lacecap flowers in early summer followed by red berries in autumn. The yellow berried form *V. o.* 'Xanthocarpum' is an attractive variant. 2.4m/8ft

Hedging Shrubs for Seaside

Shrubs need to be tolerant of wind and sometimes even of salt spray if they are planted near the sea. However, one advantage of this position is that the winter frosts are not so severe with the result that shrubs that are doubtfully hardy can thrive.

***Escallonia* 'Apple Blossom'** E: ❍
Glossy green leaves and pink and white flowers in summer make this an attractive option. Escallonias withstand wind and salt spray. 1.8m/6ft

Griselinia littoralis E
Establish in spring on a well-drained site for it is not ideally suited to cold areas. It is good on chalk. Glossy apple-green leaves, handsome in the plain or cream-variegated forms. Plant 1m/3ft apart. Prune in spring. 2.4m/8ft

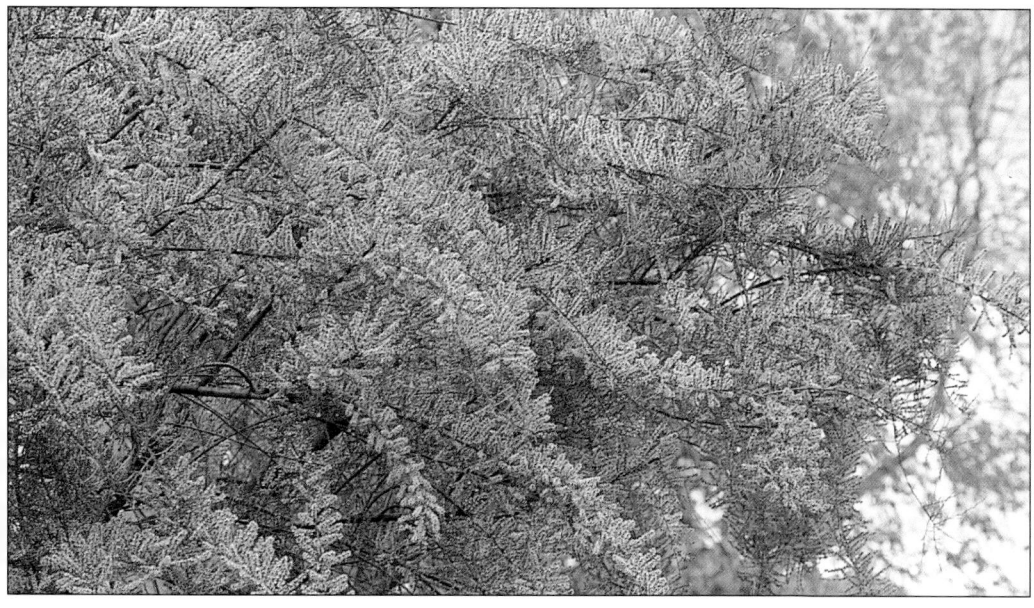

***Tamarix tetrandra* (Tamarisk)** ❍
Soft feathery glaucous scale-like foliage makes this a graceful shrub at all seasons. In early summer it becomes plumed with long clusters of tiny pink flowers. Prune after flowering. It withstands salt winds. 4m/13ft

CONSIDER ALSO:
Escallonia 'Iveyi' p.179
Fuchsia magellanica
Hebe × *franciscana* 'Blue Gem'
Hydrangea macrophylla
Olearia macrodonta p.198

Garrya elliptica E
A Californian shrub making a marvellous hedge in sheltered positions, with glaucous leaves and silvery catkins in late winter. The female's catkins are much shorter, so ensure you buy the male plant, the best clone of which is called 'James Roof'. Plant 1m/3ft apart. Prune in spring. 2.1m/7ft

Low Dividers

CONSIDER ALSO:

Hyssopus officinalis p.189
Salvia officinalis p.115
Rosmarinus officinalis 'Miss Jessop's Upright' (syn. 'Fastigiatus') p.115

All low dividers are only for use in cultivated areas, otherwise infiltrating weeds will soon overpower them. They vary in height from a few inches to 1.2m/4ft. They cannot be used for screening, but are excellent for edges, to provide a frame, or even a pattern within whose outline different plants can be grown (on the model of the old knot gardens).

***Buxus sempervirens* 'Suffruticosa'** E
The edging box which can be kept clipped to a few centimetres. Plant 15cm/6in apart and trim in early summer, and again if needed in autumn. 30cm/1ft

Cotoneaster horizontalis
The fish-bone cotoneaster can make an unusual informal low hedge with a spraying habit if it is grown against a support which it can drape over. 75cm/2½ft

***Fagus sylvatica* 'Atropurpurea' (Purple-leafed beech)**
A lovely hedge with glossy dark leaves which would form an excellent backdrop to a red border. 1m/3ft upwards

Lavandula in variety (**Lavender**) E: ❍
L. angustifolia 'Hidcote' will make a low dense aromatic hedge of grey foliage with violet flowers in summer. 45cm/1½ft. 'Grappenhall', Dutch lavender with paler purple spikes, will reach 1.2m/4ft in flower.

***Ligustrum ovalifolium* 'Aureum' (Golden privet)**
Semi-E
This small-leafed shrub will require trimming several times a year to keep it low and compact. Its gold foliage makes a bright cheerful hedge. Height as required.

Lonicera nitida E
A tiny-leafed evergreen which grows fast and will therefore require several clips a year to keep it neat and dense. 60cm–1.5m/2–5ft

***Santolina chamaecyparissus* (Cotton lavender)** E: ❍
This makes a low dense hedge of pale grey foliage that withstands clipping well. Cut before the yellow bobble flowers are produced in summer. 45cm/1½ft

Hedges for Borders

Any hedge which is used to back a border should be a variety which lends itself to formal clipping. Other factors matter too. Its roots should not be unduly invasive and greedy. Its width is important: a slim border needs a slim hedge; a larger border can share its space with a corpulent hedge like yew. Colour can be another consideration, for the purple-leafed varieties are sometimes used to provide a contrast to pale flowers before them. One practical factor is especially important; as a general rule, confine yourself to those hedges which need only one annual clip. It is a major drawback not only to prune but pick up the fallen twigs at the back of a border more than once a year.

This elegant treatment of a narrow border backed by a hedge shows how effective the simple contrast of vertical and horizontal lines can be. The globular heads of the ornamental onion, *Allium aflatunense*, break up the straight lines of the box hedge in front and the full-size backing hedge.

A yew hedge with an arch forms the background to a foam of herbaceous plants, including the white *Epilobium angustifolium album* which shines out againt the darkness of the yew behind.

Pleached Alleys

Pleached alleys form a similar galleried walk to pergolas, but their actual structure differs in that it is formed from trees or large shrubs trained over strong wires, iron hoops or timber frames so that the tops of the plants interlace. Hawthorn was a favourite medieval subject; hornbeam, elm and lime attained later popularity; yew was favoured for the darkest of evergreen tunnels. In this century, laburnum has been a first choice to make this formal type of passage, its golden racemes weeping down within the framework in early summer. But hooped cordons of apple trees are almost as lovely in blossom, and also decorative when fruiting.

The simplest form of topiary is the stilt hedge. For this purpose, standard hornbeams or limes with clear stems to 1.8m/6ft are usually planted – firmly staked with a strong bamboo tied to the stake, extending the vertical line. Three or four stout horizontal bamboos are lashed to that and the trees branches trained to these lines.

The idea of a tunnel made of golden laburnums has become very popular in recent years. Its great advantage is that it is showy, quick-growing and easily trained. The commonly planted form which has long flower-chains is *Laburnum × watereri* 'Vossii'. All parts are poisonous.

Topiary

Nothing can equal topiary in making a garden memorable and individual, yet this living sculpture can be designed and executed without difficulty. The choice of design, however, needs thought, for it can make a garden dramatic, dignified or absurd.

Very hardy evergreens with smallish leaves and a dense habit of growth are best and will ease the gardener's lot if the plants grow slowly enough to require no more than an annual clip. The ideal subject is *Taxus baccata* (yew, below left) but *Buxus* (box, below right) is almost as good, even for intricate shapes. Consider also *Laurus nobilis* (bay laurel) in mild areas, *Prunus lusitanica* (Portugal laurel), pyracantha, *Ilex* (holly) and *Viburnum tinus* for simple shapes.

Deciduous plants like *Fagus* (beech), *Carpinus* (hornbeam) and *Crataegus × monogyna* (hawthorn) can be trained to form useful doorways and apertures in a hedge.

Training topiary shapes
To make a design, allow the shoots of the plant to grow on until they are long enough to train. You can tie them with tarred string to a bamboo or a wire framework which will form the design. Alternatively, you could make a light wooden frame of lattice-work and the small plant's new growth can be trimmed close to the frame. Clip the trained shrub or tree at the season suggested in the text describing the plant, or in late summer if not specified.

You can use either hand or electric shears for small-leafed subjects like yew and box, but secateurs are preferable for larger-leafed plants such as holly or bay whose leaves would be spoilt without individual attention. Don't clip for at least a year after planting and never clip if the branch can be trained into the shrub. Any clipping makes demands on the plant and it will need to be fed in spring with old manure or compost, bonemeal or liquid manure to keep it in peak condition.

Doorways
Although not necessarily ornamental in themselves, doorways are admirable tools of design in a hedged enclosure, if two can be lined up to afford a beautiful through-view. The easiest way to make a doorway is to bend over growths from the plants either side of the aperture you have left in the planting line, until they join hands, lashing them if necessary to a horizontal bamboo.

Windows
Hedge windows are not so commonly seen, but can be a valuable frame to a fine view. They need to be trained from the beginning by pinching out new growths around the intended inner frame. Early training avoids the risks attached to cutting into the main wood which might be unavoidable if you decide to hack out a window when the hedge is mature.

Plants for the Foot of Hedges

Hedges tend to be greedy-rooted creatures and the soil immediately around them is almost certain to be dry and robbed of nutrients. In a large border beside a hedge, you can leave a space between the plants and the bottom of the hedge, but where the area is only several feet, you have little option if you wish to plant it but must confine your choice to those tough, surface-rooting subjects which will tolerate poor conditions. In sun, the most suitable plants are those which enjoy a summer baking but winter shelter, and these include a number of small bulbs. In shade, only those plants which will thrive in dry shade are possibilities.

The hedge bottom must be weed-free before you establish any of the plants. Even though most are tough survivors, it is too much to expect them to cope with hedge roots *and* weeds.

Allium moly
Rather invasive, small ornamental onion with glaucous leaves and golden flowers in summer. For sun or shade. Many other small alliums are also suitable in sun, including the pink, *A. ostrowskianum*. Both 20cm/8in

Narcissi and **daffodils**
The stronger growing cultivars are particularly useful in front of a dark evergreen hedge such as yew here. Suitable forms might include 'Ice Follies', a white narcissus with a pale lemon cup fading to white; or the yellow daffodil 'Golden Harvest'. 45cm/1½ft or less

Species tulips ❍
Graceful bulbs most of which need a summer baking to thrive. If their position is hot and well drained, they can be left to naturalize. Suitable varieties include *Tulipa sprengeri* (above), the last tulip to flower, in early summer and worth waiting for. Its scarlet flowers, buff on the outside, look very handsome in front of a dark leafed hedge like purple beech or prunus. It will also tolerate part-shade. 45cm/1½ft

***Ornithogalum umbellatum* (Star of Bethlehem)**
A small bulb with grassy leaves and starry white flowers in late spring. It will spread happily along the bottom of a hedge. 20cm/8in

Other suitable varieties of tulip include the yellow *T. sylvestris* and *T. tarda*, a good naturalizer.

Anthemis punctata subsp. ***cupaniana*** E: ❍
White daisy flowers most of the summer over mounds of cut silver leaves. Makes a rampant carpeter but must have full sun. 30 × 45cm/1 × 1½ft

Aquilegia vulgaris **(Columbine)**
The wild aquilegia has pendent flowers in early summer which are usually purple but can be white or pink. It will self-seed happily. 60 × 30cm/2 × 1ft

Dryopteris filix-mas **(Male fern)** ◐ ●
A handsome deciduous fern which forms the shape of a shuttlecock as it matures. A strong grower in shade. It prefers moist soil but will tolerate dry. 1.2 × 1m/4 × 3ft

Galium odoratum
The sweet woodruff is spreading and tolerant of dry shade. White starry flower heads in early summer with the scent of new-mown hay. 15 × 30cm/6in × 1ft

Euphorbia robbiae E
Very spreading but handsome shrubby perennial with dark evergreen rosettes of leaves and, in spring to early summer, sprays of lime-green bracts rising to 60cm/2ft. Sun or shade. Plant 30cm/1ft apart, but the spread is indefinite.

Geranium pratense **(Meadow cranesbill)**
Native plant with violet-blue flowers in early summer and leaves colouring well in autumn. Lusty spreader and self-sowing. 60/2ft H and W

***Hebe pinguifolia* 'Pagei'** E:○
A prostrate shrub with tiny blue-grey evergreen leaves and white flowers in early summer, making excellent ground-cover. 15 × 45cm/6in × 1½ft

Lamium maculatum E: ◐
Forms a spreading carpet of green-margined, silver-splashed foliage with pink flowers in early to mid-summer. 10 × 40cm/4in × 1ft 4in. (See also *L. galeobdolon* 'Florentinum' on page 113.)

***Lunaria annua* 'Alba Variegata' (Honesty)**
A biennial but self-sowing. The white variegated form of honesty with cream-splashed leaves and flowers in early summer, followed by silvery, papery seed-heads. 75 × 30cm/2½ × 1ft

Meconopsis cambrica
Invasively self-sowing but delicately pretty yellow or orange summer-flowering Welsh poppy. Both single and double forms exist, though the latter can only be propagated by division. Sun or shade. 30 x 22cm/ 1ft × 9in

***Osteospermum jucundum* (African daisy)** ❍
Dark-eyed, lilac-pink daisy flowers with grey-blue undersides produced over many months from early summer onwards. Makes spreading mats of narrow leaves. Not reliably hardy and needs full sun. Up to 30cm/1ft H and W

***Myrrhis odorata* (Sweet Cicely)**
The ferny leaves of this herb appear early in the year and die back late. Small white flowers appear in summer. It will self-sow unless these are cut off before going to seed. 60cm/2ft H and W

Phuopsis stylosa (syn. *Crucianella stylosa*) ❍
Small rounded heads of minute pink flowers in early summer above narrow, pointed leaves, forming a mat. 20 × 45cm/8in × 1½ft

Pentaglottis sempervirens **(Alkanet)**
The bright azure flowers in late spring of this wild perennial with its coarse leaves are suitable in front of an informal hedge. 75 × 30cm/2½ × 1ft

Persicaria campanulata
A spreading, shallow-rooting plant with pale pink, sweet-scented flower heads produced over a long season from summer to autumn. Sun or shade. 75 × 60cm/ 2½ × 2ft

***Polygonatum* × *hybridum* (Solomon's seal)**
Graceful, arching stems bearing fresh green, ribbed leaves and small white pendulous flowers in late spring to early summer. Spreading rootstock, even in dry shade. 75 × 30cm/2½ × 1ft

***Tanacetum vulgare* (Tansy)**
A somewhat invasive but useful flowering herb with very decorative leaves and yellow blooms in summer.
75cm/2½ft H and W

***Vinca minor* 'Burgundy'** E: ◐ ●
This distinctively coloured form of the lesser periwinkle with small dark green leaves will make near-prostrate groundcover in shady conditions. It blooms in spring but a sprinkling of flowers continues till autumn. The soil should not be too dry.
15 × 60cm/6in × 2ft

CONSIDER ALSO:

Anemone blanda p.128
Alchemilla mollis p.52
Astrantia p.161
Bergenia cordifolia p.52
Brunnera macrophylla p.92
Campanula poscharskyana p.140
Chionodoxa
Crocus p.135
Epimedium p.104
Euphorbia cyparissias p.112
Foxgloves p.112
Hellebores p.113
Iberis sempervirens p.47
Iris foetidissima p.113
Nerine bowdenii p.134
Primroses p.111
Pulmonaria p.137
Mossy saxifrages p.47
Saxifraga × *urbium* p.175
Valerian p.116
Veronica prostrata p.97
Viola

Screens

Screening shrubs and trees are usually planted for one of three purposes: to hide an eyesore; to act as a windbreak; or to give privacy to a garden. Plants required for the first purpose should be evergreen and ornamental – bamboos are excellent subjects, though even they tend to look tatty in a hard winter. Taller eyesores can be effectively blocked with grouped conifers, not in a line but staggered.

For use as a windbreak, trees can be evergreen or deciduous, but must be thoroughly hardy inland or, if by the sea, able to endure salt gales. Many are ultimately large and quite unsuited to the smaller garden, though the *Crataegus* species and cotoneaster are useful here, as are the hollies (*Ilex*) mentioned on pages 65 and 198. Screens planted for privacy are best selected from the evergreens listed below or under Evergreen Hedges (pages 196–9). If the latter, planting distances must be increased.

Bamboos

Fargesia (syn. *Arundinaria*) ***nitida*** E
A most decorative clump-former with narrow green leaves on arching canes giving a very dainty appearance, especially when frosted, as shown here. Needs protection from wind. 4m/13ft

Pseudosasa (syn. *Arundinaria*) ***japonica*** E: ◐
A common, very hardy bamboo tolerating windswept positions. It makes a dense screen to 4.5m/15ft, with deep green canes and leaves up to 30cm/1ft long, rich green above, part grey below. Spreads by rhizomes and sometimes invasive. Better in part-shade.

Useful Screening Shrubs

Rhododendron ponticum E: LH: ◐
The common rhododendron with mauve flowers in late spring. It needs acid soil and self-sows and layers where suited. Bushy and spreading. Toxic to stock. Plant 1m/3ft apart. 3m/10ft

Viburnum tinus E
A shrub with dark, shiny leaves and pinkish-white flower clusters in winter. Plant 60cm/2ft apart and trim after flowering is finished in spring. 3m/10ft

Evergreen Windbreak Trees

Pinus nigra E
The dense, burly Austrian pine with very dark stiff needles and cones up to 7.5cm/3in long. First-class windbreak. Good even in chalky soil, but it is only suited to large gardens. 30m/100ft

Pinus radiata E: LH
The rapid-growing Monterey pine with bright green needles up to 15cm/6in long and cones up to 12cm/5in. Picturesque but generally better suited to milder, large gardens only. 30m/100ft

Deciduous Windbreak Trees

Crataegus species
Many thorn-trees are ornamental and all are tough, bushy-headed, tolerant of any soil and situation and suitable for small gardens. *C × prunifolia* has dark, glossy green leaves turning red in autumn when it also bears dark red fruit. 5m/16ft

Quercus cerris
The Turkey oak is slender and open when young, domed when old and has dark green leaves. Good in maritime exposure rather than inland. Very rapid growth to 35m/116ft and only for large gardens.

Consider also:
Acer pseudoplatanus p.236
Alnus glutinosa
Cotoneaster × watereri
Populus alba
P. tremula
P. 'Robusta'

Climbers

Climbing plants support themselves, whether by aerial roots or by adhesive pads or by twining stems (or leaf stems) or by spines on their long arching shoots which hook into and over objects in their path. Others are not strictly speaking climbers, but will shove and lean their way up a wall, or can be trained by securing their stems to wires or trellis. All these different types are indispensable for hiding unsightly boundaries or buildings, whether walls, fences, screens or sheds. Festoon these eyesores with colour and foliage, and you have a vertical garden instead. Climbers are also key plants for providing privacy, and if they are grown against a trellis or netting erected above a low wall, they will give a high degree of seclusion. Plan their position carefully, relating their ultimate height and vigour of growth to the situation they will occupy. This is important, because it is not so simple to rid yourself of a mistake when the plant has covered the wall.

Clematis armandii E: ❍
Trifoliate leaves and scented flowers in spring which are white in the form 'Snowdrift' and blush in the cultivar 'Apple Blossom'. Vigorous to 4m/13ft but a sheltered, sunny wall is essential. Provide support.

***Fremontodendron* 'Californian Glory'** E: ❍
A fast-growing plant with beautiful golden cupped flowers produced from spring through until autumn. Its lobed leaves are felted beneath with rusty down. Not a climber but best placed against a sunny wall. Not fully hardy. 5m/16ft

***Hedera colchica* 'Sulphur Heart' (Ivy)** E
A large-leafed handsome form with a golden central splash to the leaf. It is self-clinging and suitable for growing on a wall but, as with all ivies, it is sensible to ensure that the wall is sound and cannot be damaged by the ivy. 4.5m/15ft

***Lonicera japonica* 'Halliana' (Honeysuckle)** E or semi-E
A rampant climber with fragrant white, ageing to yellow, flowers from summer to autumn. It needs support and firm pruning. 10m/33ft

Trachelospermum asiaticum E: ○
A dense, self-clinging climber with evergreen leaves and creamy, fragrant, jasmine-like flowers in later summer. Needs a warm wall. Rather slow. 6m/20ft

CLIMBERS: LARGE-FLOWERED CLEMATIS

Clematis are an immensely varied group, all of which need their roots shaded to thrive. Plant the root ball 5cm/2½in deeper than the soil level in the pot to protect against wilt, and tie stems to wall support.

***C.* 'Ernest Markham'**
A valuable climber which has carmine flowers and yellow anthers in late summer. It is a very vigorous hybrid. 3–4m/10–13ft

***C.* 'Perle d'Azur'**
A late-flowering variety which bears azure blue blooms from summer to early autumn. 3–4m/10–13ft

See also *C.* 'Jackmanii Superba' on p. 148.

***C.* 'Nelly Moser'**
This popular form gives a prolific display of pale mauve flowers with a deeper bar in early summer and a secondary show in late summer. 3–4m/10–13ft

***C.* 'Marie Boisselot'** (syn. 'Madame le Coultre')
A dazzling clematis bearing very large white flowers with yellow anthers from summer onwards. It will grow vigorously in sun or shade. 3–4m/10–13ft

C. alpina
Early spring-flowering, blue in the type, though there is a purplish-pink form shown here, called 'Ruby' and a double white cultivar ('White Moth'). 3m/10ft

C. macropetala
This species blooms in spring. The blue 'Maidwell Hall' is shown here. It looks at its prettiest beside the pink cultivar 'Markham's Pink', also shown. 3m/10ft

C. montana rubens
This very vigorous plant flowers in late spring, growing to 10m/33ft. The white form, *C. montana*, is equally rampant.

***C.m.* 'Tetrarose'**
This montana clematis is less vigorous and bears rosy-lilac flowers and bronzed foliage.

CLIMBERS: CLEMATIS SPECIES

The late-flowering species clematis are both beautiful and useful, prolonging the season of colour. They are usually hard pruned in late winter or earliest spring and will make vigorous growth in the next few months to flower from the second half of the summer into autumn.

See also *Clematis cirrhosa balearica* on p.138 and *Clematis armandii* p.222.

***Clematis orientalis* (Orange-peel clematis)**
A late-flowering species with thickly textured lantern-shaped yellow sepals and fluffy silvery seed-heads. 'Bill MacKenzie' is a good form and more vigorous than the type. 4m/13ft

Clematis tangutica
A late-flowering species with nodding yellow bells which are followed by silky silvery seed-heads, attractive in their own right. Vigorous to 5m/16ft

C. viticella
The viticella clematis bloom in summer to autumn. The deepest purple form is 'Royal Velours', shown here growing over a pink *Lavatera*. There is also a white, green-tipped form called 'Alba Luxurians'. 'Rubra' with wine-red flowers is equally good. 3m/10ft

***C. viticella* 'Purpurea Plena Elegans'**
A double viticella clematis which bears a large number of blooms over a long period. 3m/10ft

Of the easily obtainable cultivars, the roses shown here are fine representatives of the different colour ranges. Tie all to supports on a wall.

***R.* 'Guinée'** ❍
A very velvety deep red rose, almost black as a bud, with a powerful scent. A vigorous climber but only once flowering. 6m/20ft

***R.* 'Lady Waterlow'**
A climbing rose of the hybrid tea type with lovely lightly scented flowers produced freely in early summer, with a second scattering in late summer. 3.5m/12ft

***R.* 'Mermaid'** ❍
Loveliest of the yellows with large, single flowers all summer and semi-evergreen leaves. Needs ample space and a sheltered wall. Do not prune. 9m/30ft

***R.* 'Mme. Alfred Carrière'**
A sweetly scented and perpetual flowering rose with double blush-white flowers and disease-free foliage. Also good for north walls. 6m/20ft

***R.* 'New Dawn'**
This apple-scented rose has recurrent-flowering, flesh-pink blooms and dark, glossy leaves which are very healthy. 4m/13ft

***R.* 'Mme. Grégoire Staechelin'**
Once-blooming only in early summer but has an impressive display of large, scented pink flowers, crimson in bud. Large hips follow. 7m/23ft

Consider also the rapid climbers shown on page 150: *Cobaea scandens, Ipomoea, Lathyrus odoratus,* Nasturtium, *Thunbergia alata*

Actinidia kolomikta ❍
Slow to start, but very striking when established on a sunny wall, this climber's leaves are often part-pink or white. 4m/13ft

Akebia quinata Semi-E: ❍
A vigorous and unusual climber with dusky purple vanilla-scented flowers in late spring followed by purplish brown sausages. Light-green foliage. For a warm position. 9m/10ft

Passiflora caerulea Semi-E: ❍
The beautiful and rampant, blue and white-flowered passion flower, blossoming in summer-autumn, when it produces orange fruits. There is a fine white form called 'Constance Elliot'. 6m/20ft

***Campsis* × *tagliabuana* 'Madame Galen'** ❍
A very vigorous climber which needs support. Pinnate leaves and showy trumpet flowers in late summer. Full sun is essential for a wonderful plant giving brilliant colour late in the year. To 6m/20ft

***Solanum crispum* 'Glasnevin'** semi-E: ❍
Lanky but rapid grower with semi-evergreen leaves and violet flowers with a yellow staminal beak, borne in clusters all summer. Give it firm support against a wall. 5m/16ft

Vitis coignetiae ❍
A rampant, ornamental vine with big leaves, turning crimson in autumn in the best forms. Give it plenty of space for it will cover a high house wall, given support. Ultimately up to 20m/66ft

***Vitis vinifera* 'Purpurea'** ❍
The black grapes of this vine are inedible and it is grown only for its foliage. The new olive green leaves turn dark red, then purple. 4m/13ft

Wisteria floribunda ❍
Arguably the noblest of all climbers with 60cm/2ft long trusses of scented pea-flowers. In the form 'Macrobotrys' they reach 1m/3ft long but the upper flowers tend to have died off before the lower ones open. 5m/16ft

Wisteria sinensis ❍
This lovely climber is a very vigorous grower with mauve flowers in early summer. White and pink forms are obtainable also, and there is a double purple variety called 'Black Dragon'. The flowering racemes are about 25cm/10in long. 30m/100ft

***Hedera helix* 'Angularis Aurea'** E: ◐
A decorative golden ivy whose colour lightens a part-shady corner, though its yellow will fade if it receives no sun. Self-clinging. 4m/13ft

***Hydrangea anomala petiolaris* (Climbing hydrangea)** ◐ ●
Although this plant climbs with aerial roots, give it support when young. White flowers in lacy corymbs in summer. Moist, leafy soil. 6m/20ft

Parthenocissus henryana ◐ ●
A beautiful self-clinging climber with bronze-green pale-veined leaves in summer that turn to crimson velvet in autumn. 9m/30ft

Schizophragma integrifolium ◐
The large flower-heads of this self-clinging climber are borne in summer and surrounded by showy white bracts. Like the climbing hydrangea, it can be slow to get going and will benefit from help and a humus-rich soil. 12m/39ft

Pergolas and Arbours

Pergolas originated in Italy where they were used as a method of growing vines until it became apparent how decoratively they could support all manner of climbing plants. Usually made from stone, brick or timber piers topped by horizontal cross-beams, they make cool, airy pathways, partly shaded in summer by their canopy of abundant foliage and flowers. At one extreme they can be installed in prosaic surroundings connecting, for example, a garage with a house door; or, shown at their most enchanting, they can form a canopy to a small bridge across water, the whole graceful structure reflected in the stream. Bowers or arbours are the simplest to make of these ornamental features, just summerhouses formed from climbing plants trained to cover and weep over a structure of iron or timber. The most inviting spot to build an arbour is in the sunshiny nook made between two walls, so long as it faces an engaging view.

CLIMBERS FOR PERGOLAS AND ARBOURS

Suitable plants are to be found in the following list. Always relate their habit to the size of the structure they must festoon.

Clematis in variety p.224
Hedera (ivy) in variety
Humulus lupulus 'Aureus' p.62
Jasminum officinale p.148
Lonicera (honeysuckle) in variety p.47
Solanum crispum 'Glasnevin' p.229
Vitis 'Brant'
Vitis coignetiae p.230
Vitis vinifera purpurea p.230
Wisteria sinensis p.230
Wisteria floribunda p.230

Climbing roses need choosing with care since they need to be flexible. Also most are too tall for the verticals and will flower out of sight at the top but the following are suitable.

R. 'Albertine'
R. 'Bleu Magenta'
R. 'Blush Noisette'
R. 'New Dawn'

***Rosa* 'Albertine'**
An old favourite and a robust rambler which produces a mass of double salmon-pink flowers in summer. Better on a pergola than a wall as it is liable to mildew in a dry position. 5m/15ft

***Rosa* 'Bleu Magenta'**
A sumptuously dark rambling rose with small very double flowers which look wonderful hanging in garlands along a pergola in high summer. 4.5m/15ft

***Rosa* 'Blush Noisette'**
A very pretty climbing noisette for a sheltered position. It produces fairly continuous flowers in summer and as it is short-growing, is ideal for a small arbour. 2.1m/7ft

Climbers and their Hosts

One of the most elegant ways of cultivating climbing plants is to grow them in layers. A robust, mature, stiff host plant supports a more fragile, lanky climbing plant, and in a small garden it is an ideal way of introducing diversity, for two or even three plants are grown over the same space.

Pairing the 'host' plant and its 'guest' is a matter partly of common sense, partly of knowing how each grows, and partly of aesthetic taste. Obviously both plants should enjoy the same aspect and soil. Equally obvious is the fact that the host plant should be stout and mature enough to resist being smothered by the climber enveloping it. Pair those plants which flower at different seasons and you enjoy a double display in the same area.

Possible host plants include cotoneasters, berberis, evergreens with very small leaves like yew or cypress, pyracantha, and viburnum. Trees can also be suitable, such as old, fruitless apple or pear trees which can make excellent hosts. So do many small trees whose outer branches dip low enough to the ground, so that the climber (planted at this outer perimeter, well out of range of the tree's greedy roots) can be trained to grow up this framework.

Rosa 'Paul's Himalayan Musk' festoons an old apple tree. Rambler roses like this flower only once in summer but the blooms can be so abundant that they completely cover the host.

This *Clematis montana* 'Grandiflora' looks very pretty over *Ceanothus* 'Blue Mound' but it will have to be removed. Always take care that a climber doesn't throttle its host. The clematis here will kill this ceanothus if it is allowed to remain over its branches.

Climbing roses can be both hosts and guests. An old pear tree supports *Rosa filipes* 'Kiftsgate', as a guest. This huge rambler rose grows so large it is almost uncontrollable so it can only be grown in the right circumstances.

Vitis coignetiae, which is a truly lusty climber, drapes itself over a large pine, a brilliant combination as the autumn tints of the vine leaves glow against the blue pine needles. However, a rampant climber like this might damage the tree.

This climbing rose provides the supporting framework for a clematis. Climbing roses make a stiffer framework than rambling roses.

Trees

A small tree is a substantial asset in all but the tiniest gardens, bestowing shade near a house and effecting a change of height which is always essential to engage interest. And if it can be planted to the side of the garden and allowed to overhang slightly one of the walls or fences, it will also help to dispel the feeling of claustrophobia sometimes induced by small enclosures.

Since it will be a dominant plant, the tree deserves to be chosen with care. Perhaps spectacular flowers at one season are the most important feature, or a beautifully marked bark which will look handsome throughout the year. A graceful evergreen tree may be preferable whose leaves help to keep the garden clothed at all seasons. Or instead will a tree be needed to bear edible fruit?

In larger gardens there is room for more choice about the kinds of trees and their positions. They don't have to be planted on their own as specimens. It is worth bearing in mind that small trees are often worthwhile in the shrub border where they break the bushy monotony and give extra height. Even in the large mixed or herbaceous border, they may have a part to play. One on its own can be the dominant plant around which the rest of the border is assembled. Or a number of the same species planted at even intervals will give formal regularity to the border. For this purpose the fastigiate conifers on page 246 are the most useful.

Amelanchier canadensis
LH
Dense deciduous tree with white flowers in spring, richly colouring leaves in autumn. Sometimes a shrubby habit. 6 × 3m/ 20 × 10ft

***Acer pseudoplatanus* 'Brilliantissimum'**
Slow-growing mop-head. New foliage in spring is soft salmon pink, turning to yellow-green. 6 × 7m/20 × 23ft

***Magnolia* × *loebneri* 'Leonard Messel'**
A beautiful lime-tolerant hybrid with delicate flowers on bare branches before the pale green leaves develop. 8 × 6m/26 × 20ft

Magnolia salicifolia LH
Most beautiful mass of 12cm/5in pure white scented flowers in spring on the leafless branches. Willow-like leaves. Conical habit. 10 × 5m/33 × 16ft

There is a further selection of trees in other sections:
Plants for Heavy Clay Soils pp. 16–19
Plants for Alkaline Soils pp. 26–9
Plants for Lime-free or Acid Soils pp.36–9
Gold and Green pp.64–7
Grey and Silver pp.72–3

Magnolia* × *soulangeana LH: ❍
The most popular and adaptable of the magnolias with spectacular, goblet-shaped flowers in spring before the leaves open. It is tolerant of clay soils and atmospheric pollution. There are a number of fine clones, including

'Alba' (above left). 'Lennei' (above right), 'Rustica Rubra' (the outside is rosy-crimson) and 'Brozzoni' with especially large white flowers bearing a purple stain at the base. The tree is usually rather shrubby and wide-spreading. 6m/20ft H and W

Malus floribunda
The low, bushy, very broad-headed Japanese crab-apple tree bearing masses of small flowers which are rosy-red in bud and pink fading to white when open. Small red and yellow fruits in autumn. 5 × 6m/16 × 20ft

***Malus* × *moerlandsii* 'Profusion'**
Crab apple with wine-red flowers in late spring and purple-red 2.5cm/1in fruit in autumn. Purplish juvenile foliage, ageing to bronze-green. 6 × 4m/20 × 13ft

***Prunus cerasifera* 'Pissardii'**
Soft pink flowers in very early spring, new foliage ruby red, turning heavy purple later in year. 6m/20ft H and W but sometimes clipped to a mop-head. *Prunus* × *blireana* is similar, but flowers later, bronzed leaf. 10m/33ft H and W

***Prunus* 'Amanogawa'**
Very narrow columnar habit, useful for limited spaces. Casts little shade. Semi-double, pale pink flowers in spring. 10 × 4m/33 × 13ft

***Prunus* 'Pink Shell'**
A beautiful member of a family which are all excellent subjects for limy soil. It has spreading branches and semi-double flowers opening in spring. The leaves usually colour red and orange in autumn.
9 × 8m/30 × 26ft

Cornus florida rubra ❍
Bushy, wide-spreading tree with beautiful rosy-pink bracts surrounding its flowers in early summer. But performs well only in areas with reliably warm summers.
5 × 7m/16 × 23ft

Eucryphia* × *nymansensis E
Glorious late-summer flowering tree which needs its roots shaded and some protection from cold winds. For moist, well-drained soils. It has an erect habit and tolerates a degree of alkalinity in the soil.
15 × 4m/49 × 13ft

***Halesia monticola* (Snowdrop tree)**
This spreading or conical tree, a North American native, is happier on lime-free soils. White bells hang from the underside of branches in late spring. 8 × 10m/26 × 33ft

CONSIDER ALSO:
***Prunus subhirtella* 'Autumnalis'**, a most valuable tree near a house for its winter beauty. Its delicate white (or palest pink in the form 'Rosea') bell-shaped flowers open in small, intermittent flushes from late autumn throughout the winter, the remainder blooming in spring. Spreading, densely-twigged crown. 8m/26ft H and W

Genista aetnensis ❍
A shrub with a tree-like habit. Support initially with a stake. Its green stems are almost leafless so it casts virtually no shade and is ideal for the mixed and herbaceous border. Gold flowers in summer. 5m/16ft H and W

Koelreuteria paniculata ❍
A domed, picturesque tree with branching panicles up to 45cm/1½ft long of golden flowers in late summer. Its long, dark green pinnate leaves open as deep red in late spring and turn yellow in autumn. Full sun is preferable. 10m/33ft H and W

Cornus alternifolia subsp. **'Argentea'**
The variegated pagoda dogwood, a shrubby tree, needs room for the display of its tiered pattern of branches which grow like stacked plates. Silver variegated leaves.
3 × 2.1m/10 × 7ft

Acer griseum **(Paperbark maple)** ❍
A most desirable tree with a peeling rufous bark and trifoliate leaves that turn red and gold in autumn.
8 × 6m/26 × 20ft

Eucalyptus pauciflora subsp. ***niphophila*** E: ❍
Rather gaunt, reasonably hardy, slow-growing, evergreen tree with wonderfully patterned green, grey and cream bark which should not be obscured by neighbouring plants. Casts very little shade.
10 × 8m/33 × 26ft

***Prunus pendula* 'Pendula Rosea'**
Forms an extraordinary, spreading hummock whose pendulous branches are fascinating even in winter bareness. Flowers in spring and needs a great deal of lateral space. 5 × 7m/16 × 23ft

Prunus serrula
A vigorous tree with a polished mahogany-red bark which is handsome at all times of the year. Dullish green leaves which tend to hide the mass of very small white flowers in late spring. 8m/26ft H and W

***Cotoneaster frigidus* 'Cornubia'** semi-E
Useful for its persistent red berries in autumn onwards, semi-evergreen leaf, vigour and tolerance of difficult sites, but wide-spreading and ultimately up to 7m/23ft H and W

***Arbutus unedo* (Killarney strawberry tree)** E
Darkish-red bark, dark evergreen leaves, and highly ornamental strawberry-like fruits in late autumn at the same time as the white flower-bells open. The form 'Rubra' has pinkish flowers. (The fruit is edible but unpalatable.) 5m/16ft H and W

***Malus* 'Evereste'**
Pink-white flowers mass this dwarf crab apple in spring followed by scarlet fruit in autumn. 3.5 x 2.4m/13 x 8ft. There are a number of other ornamental hybrid apples including the excellent 'Red Sentinel' whose glossy red fruits persist for months on the tree.

***Sorbus commixta* (Japanese Rowan)**
A vigorous rowan with glossy green leaves that turn purple and scarlet in autumn. The white flowers of spring are followed by clusters of brilliant orange-red berries. 10 x 5m/33 x 16ft

Sorbus hupehensis
This rowan has long silvery glaucous leaflets, orange-red in autumn. Its white yellow-centred flowers in spring are succeeded by green berries that turn white or blush pink. 13 × 8m/43 × 26ft

Sorbus sargentiana
A magnificent broad-headed rowan which makes one of the great autumn displays. Its green leaflets turn rich scarlet and gold in autumn. Its flat white inflorescences in spring are followed by large dazzling clusters of red berries. 6m/20ft H and W

Sorbus vilmorinii
A very pretty rowan though it is sometimes a weak grower. Its deeply divided leaves are a dark grey-green, reddening in late autumn. White spring flowers are followed by fruits that are notable for their charming variation in colour, starting dark rose-red, and developing in stages through pink to blush white. 4 × 5m/ 13 × 16ft

SLIM CONIFERS AND EVERGREEN TREES

These can be planted as specimen trees or used to make a narrow focal point (or series of focal points) in beds and borders.

CONSIDER ALSO:
Juniperus virginiana 'Skyrocket'
Chamaecyparis lawsoniana 'Kilmacurragh'

***Juniperus chinensis* 'Aurea'** E: ❍
A slow-growing and very slim column of golden-foliage which looks particularly handsome forming a spire in a border as here. 8 × 1.2m/26 × 4ft

***Taxus baccata* 'Fastigiata' (Irish Yew)** E
This slender form of yew is slow, makes a broad column eventually.
10 × 3m/33 × 10ft

***Juniperus communis* 'Hibernica'** E
This forms a very narrow column of blue-grey foliage and is an excellent accent subject. Its growth is slow but as it ages, it may need tying in to keep it erect.
4m × 45cm/13 × 1½ft

***Chamaecyparis lawsoniana* 'Columnaris'** E: ❍
A pencil slim conifer with blue-grey spice-scented foliage. It broadens slightly with age but will take a little clipping. 9 × 1.2m/30 × 4ft

Gingko biloba
Marvellous tree which is one of the main choices for a large garden. A deciduous conifer which is the only survivor of an important family of trees in existence 160 million years ago. Held sacred in the East and found planted by Buddhist temples. Exquisite ribbed foliage, yellowing in autumn on a columnar tree when young, which broadens with age. Slow growth. 25 × 7m/80 × 23ft

CONSIDER ALSO:
Pinus radiata p.221

Cedrus libani subsp. ***atlantica* 'Glauca' (Blue Atlas cedar)** ❍
This magnificent vigorous tree needs plenty of space in a large garden. It bears barrel-shaped cones of 7.5cm/3in. Its silvery-blue foliage, especially brilliant in spring, size and elegant conical shape make it outstanding. 16 × 9m/ 52 × 30ft

Pinus wallichiana (syns. *excelsa, griffithii*) E
Fine, fast-growing and fairly adaptable pine, though not for shallow chalk, with blue-grey-green needles, 20cm/8in long, and curving cones which can be yet longer. Soft, almost feathery appearance. 15 × 10m/ 50 × 33ft

Picea breweriana E
Another very beautiful conifer called 'Brewer's Weeping Spruce', which is hung with deep green curtains of 60cm/2ft long branchlets. Slow growing. 10 × 7m/33 × 23ft

Index

Abelia schumannii 16
Abies koreana 49
Abutilon 151
  A. × *suntense* 178
  A. vitifolium 178
Acaena 35
  A. 'Blue Haze' 70, 98
Acanthus spinosus 35, 54, 114
Acer griseum 242
  A. palmatum 'Dissectum Atropurpureum' 90, 125
  A. p. 'Dissectum' 88, 89, 90
  A. platanoides 'Drummondii' 18
  A. pseudoplatanus 'Brilliantissimum' 18, 221, 236
  A. shirasawanum f. *aureum* 63
Achillea filipendulina 'Gold Plate' 30
  A. 'The Beacon' 30
Aconitum napellus 20
Actinidia kolomikta 228
Adiantum pedatum 40
  A. venustum 40
Aesculus parviflora 16
African daisy, see *Arctotis*
African lily, see *Agapanthus*
Agapanthus 'Headbourne Hybrids' 160
Agave americana 'Marginata' 151
Ajuga 25, 111
  A. reptans 'Pink Surprise' 104
  A. r. 'Burgundy Glow' 104
Akebia quinata 228
Alchemilla mollis 25, 52, 105, 113, 219
Algerian iris, see *I. unguicularis*
Alkanet, see *Pentaglottis*
Allium 35, 114
  A. aflatunense 132, 208
  A. a. 'Purple Sensation' 132
  A. christophii 132
  A. moly 212
  A. ostrowskianum 212
Alnus glutinosa 18, 221
Alstroemeria 'Ligtu Hybrids' 166
Alum root, see *Heuchera*
Alyssum saxatile 30
  A. spinosum roseum 100
Amaranthus caudatus 151
Amelanchier canadensis 236
Anagallis monellii 154
Anchusa azurea 'Loddon Royalist' 166
Androsace lanuginosa 94, 103
Andromeda polifolia 'Compacta' 36
Anemone blanda 35, 128, 219
  A. × *hybrida* 25, 144, 165
  A. × *hybrida* 'September Charm' 144
  A. nemorosa 128
Angelica 188
Angel's fishing rod, see *Dierama*
Angel's trumpet, see *Brugmansia*
Annual cornflower, see *Centaurea*
Antennaria dioica 'Rosea' 70, 98, 103
  A. aprica 98
Anthemis cupaniana 70, 114, 173, 214
Anthericum liliago 30
Anthriscus sylvestris 'Ravenswing' 90
Antirrhinum 154
Apple 209, 234, and see *Malus*
Aquilegia 'Snow Queen' 160
  A. vulgaris 214
Arabis 35
Aralia elata 18
  A. e. 'Variegata' 92
Arbutus unedo 127, 244
Arctotis × *hybrida* 154
Armeria 114
  A. maritima 94
Artemesia abrotanum 85
  A. absinthium 'Lambrook Silver' 68, 165
  A. canescens 172
  A. 'Powis Castle' 88
  A. ludoviciana 68
Aruncus dioicus 'Kneiffii' 160
Asarina 'Victoria Falls' 153
Ash, see *Fraxinus*
Asperula odorata 113
Asphodeline lutea 31
Asplenium scolopendrium 110
  A. trichomanes 31
Aster × *frikartii* 145, 161
  A. novi-belgii 'Harrison's Blue 20
  A. sedifolius (syn. *acris*) 20
Astilbe 111, 161, 187
  A. 'Erica' 161
Astrantia 25, 111, 161, 219
  A. major 161
  A. maxima 161
Athyrium filix-femina 53, 174
  A. f.-f. plumosum 53
  A. f.-f. 'Victoriae' 53
Aubrieta deltoidea 31, 103
Aucuba japonica 196
  A. 'Gold Dust' 18, 63
Auricula, see *Primula auricula*
Autumn crocus, see *Colchicum*
Azalea 39, 51
Azara lanceolata 48, 79

Ballota pseudodictamnus 176
Balsam fir, see *Abies balsamea*
Bamboo, see *Fargesia* and *Pseudosasa*
Barberry, see *Berberis*
Bay 188, 210
Bear's breeches, see *Acanthus spinosus*
Beauty bush, see *Kolkwitzia*
Beech, see *Fagus*
Begonia semperflorens 145, 154
Bellflower, see *Campanula*
Berberis 18, 234
  B. darwinii 120
  B. stenophylla 196
  B. thunbergii 'Aurea' 63
  B. t. 'Rose Glow' 90
  Bergamot, see *Monarda*
Bergenia 25, 105, 113, 165

B. 'Ballawley' 52
B. cordifolia 52
B. c. 'Purpurea' 52
B. 'Silberlicht' 52
Betula albo-sinensis 16
B. ermanii 16
Birch, see *Betula*
Bistort, see *Persicaria bistorta*
Black mulberry, see *Morus nigra*
Blechnum tabulare 43, 88
Bleeding heart, see *Dicentra spectabilis*
Blue Atlas cedar, see *Cedrus libani* subsp. *atlantica* 'Glauca'
Blue marguerite, see *Felicia amelloides*
Blue oat grass, see *Helichtotrichon*
Bog rosemary, see *Andromeda*
Borage 188
Bottle Brush, see *Callistemon*
Bowles' golden sedge, see *Carex elata* 'Aurea'
Box 196, and see *Buxus*
Brachyglottis 'Sunshine' 72
Brewers weeping spruce, see *Picea breweriana*
Bridal wreath, see *Spiraea* 'Arguta'
Brompton stock, see *Matthiola*
Brugmansia 79, 151
Brunnera macrophylla 25, 165, 219
B.m. 'Variegata' 92
Buddleja alternifolia 26
B. crispa 72, 178
B. davidii 79, 124, 180
B. d. 'Dartmoor' 26, 180
B. d. 'Nanho Blue' 72
B. globosa 74
B. 'Lochinch' 72
Buphthalmum, see *Telekia*
Busy Lizzie, see *Impatiens*
Buxus sempervirens 210
B. s. 'Handsworthiensis' 196
B. s. 'Suffruticosa' 206

Calico bush, see *Kalmia*
Californian poppy, see *Eschscholzia*
Callicarpa bodinieri var *giraldii* 126
Callistemon citrinus 'Splendens' 39
C. rigidus 178
Calluna vulgaris 'Silver Knight' 36
Caltha palustris 25
C. p. 'Flore Pleno' 182
Camassia 25
C. leichtlinii 132
Camellia 39, 50
C. 'Galaxie' 120
C. japonica 50
C. 'Leonard Messel' 50
C. 'Nobilissima' 138
C. sasanqua 'Narumigata' 138
C. × *williamsii* 50
Campanula 35
C. alliariifolia 172
C. 'Birch Hybrid' 100
C. cochleariifolia 96
C. garganica 31, 103
C. glomerata 'Superba' 32
C. lactiflora 166
C latiloba 20
C. persicifolia 35
C. p. 'Telham Beauty' 144
C. portenschlagiana 140
C. poscharskyana 96, 219
Campsis 229
Candytuft, see *Iberis umbellatum*
Caragana arborescens 'Lorbergii' 26
Cardoon, see *Cynara*
Carex 175
C. comans 86
C. elata 'Aurea' 60
Carpenteria californica 50, 79, 122, 179
Carpinus betulus 18, 200, 209, 210
Cassiope 'Muirhead' 36, 103
Caster oil plant, see *Ricinus*
Catalpa bignonioides 'Aurea' 67
Catmint, see *Nepeta* × *faassenii*
Ceanothus 50, 79, 121, 179, 234
C. 'Autumnal Blue' 50
C. 'Burkwoodii' 50
C. 'Cascade' 50
C. 'Delight' 50
C. impressus 'Puget Blue' 50
C. 'Trewithen Blue' 179
Cedrus libani subsp. *atlantica* 'Glauca' 247
Centaurea cyanus 32
C. hypoleuca 'John Coutts' 145, 161
Centranthus 219
C. ruber 116
Cerastium 114
C. tomentosum 'Silver Carpet' 70, 98
Ceratostigma plumbaginoides 106
Cercis siliquastrum 27
Chaenomeles speciosa 'Nivalis' 17
C. × *superba* 'Crimson and Gold' 201
C. × *s.* 'Pink Lady' 180
C. × *s.* 'Rowallane' 201
Chamaecyparis lawsoniana 196
C. l. 'Columnaris' 246
C. l. 'Ellwoodii' 196
C. l. 'Kilmacurragh' 246
Chamaemelum nobile 84
C. 'Treneague' 84
Cheiranthus 80
Cherry Tree, see *Prunus*
Cherry pie, see *Heliotropium*
Chervil 188
Chimonanthus fragrans 79
Chinese lantern, see *Physalis*
Chinese witch hazel, see *Hamamelis*
Chionodoxa 219
C. luciliae 129
Chocolate vine, see *Akebia*
Choisya ternata 18, 48, 179
C. 'Aztec Pearl' 74
C. 'Sundance' 64
Christmas box, see *Sarcococca*
Chrysanthemum, see *Dendranthema*
Chusan palm, see *Trachycarpus fortunei*
Cistus 179
C. × *cyprius* 51, 122
C. 'Peggy Sammons' 51, 122
C. × *pulverulentus* 51, 114
C. × *purpureus* 51, 122
Clematis 232, 235
C. alpina 225
C. a. 'Ruby' 225
C. a. 'White Moth' 225
C. armandii 79, 222
C. a. 'Apple Blossom' 222
C .a. 'Snowdrift' 222
C. cirrhosa var. *balearica* 79, 138
C. 'Ernest Markham' 224
C. 'Jackmanii Superba' 148, 224
C. macropetala 'Markham's Pink' 225
C. m. 'Maidwell Hall' 225
C. 'Madame le Coultre' 224
C. 'Marie Boisselot', see *C.* 'Madame Le Coultre'
C. montana 225
C. m. rubens 225
C. m. 'Tetrarose' 225
C. 'Nelly Moser' 224
C. orientalis 'Bill Mackenzie' 226
C. 'Perle d'Azur' 226
C. tangutica 226
C. viticella 'Alba Luxurians' 226
C. v. 'Purpurea Plena Elegans' 226
C. v. 'Royal Velours' 226

C. v. 'Rubra' 226
Cleome 145
Clianthus puniceus 179
Clover, see *Trifolium*
Cobaea scandens 149, 150, 228
Colchicum autumnale 134
Columbine 214, and see *Aquilegia*
Comfrey, see *Symphytum*
Convallaria majalis 80
Convolvulus cneorum 70
Cordyline australis 56
C. a 'Atropurpurea' 91
Coreopsis verticillata 35, 144
Cornflower, see *Centaurea*
Cornus alba 'Aurea' 64
C. a. 'Elegantissima' 92
C. alternifolia 'Argentea' 242
C. canadensis 39, 104
C. florida rubra 240
C. kousa var. *chinensis* 126
Corylopsis pauciflora 39, 138
Corylus 18
Cosmos astrosanguineus 81, 145, 154
Cotinus coggygria 17
C. c. 'Royal Purple' 90
Cotoneaster 18, 234
C. dammeri 106
C. franchettii 197
C. frigidus 'Cornubia' 127, 244
C. horizontalis 180, 206
C. lacteus 197
C. salicifolius 'Exburyensis' 126
C. × *watereri* 221
Cotton lavender, see *Santolina*
Crab apple 234, and see *Malus*
Cranesbill, see *Geranium*
Crassula sarcocaulis 101
Crataegus × *monogyna* 18, 200, 210
C. × *prunifolia* 221
Crinum × *powellii* 82, 134
Crocosmia 132
C. 'Citronella' 54
C. 'Lucifer' 54
C. masoniorum 25
Crocus 35, 135, 219
C. chrysanthus 'Bluebird 135
C. c. 'Blue Pearl' 135
C. c. 'Zenith' 135
C. tommasinianus 135
C. t. 'Whitewell Purple' 135
Crown imperial, see *Fritillaria imperialis*
× *Cupressocyparis leylandii* 197
C. l. 'Castlewellan' 197
Currant, see *Ribes*
Curry plant, see *Helichrysum angustifolium*
Cyclamen coum 103, 136
C. hederifolium 135
Cynara 114
C. cardunculus 56, 70
C. scolymus 56
Cypress 234
Cystisus battandieri 72, 79, 179
C. × *kewensis* 106

Daffodil 212, and see *Narcissus*
Dahlia 145
D. merckii 170
Daphne × *burkwoodii* 'Somerset' 75
D. cneorum 'Eximia' 75, 103
D. mezereum 138
D. m. 'Alba' 138
D. odora 'Aureomarginata' 79, 138
D. pontica 177
Darmera peltata 182
Datura, see *Brugmansia*
Day Lily 82, 163, and see *Hemerocallis*
Dead nettle, see *Lamium*
Delphinium Belladonna varieties 167
Dendranthema 'Ruby Mound' 167
Deutzia × *elegantissima* 'Rosealind' 27
D. setchuenensis corymbiflora 124
Dianthus 82
D. arenarius 70
D. barbatus 81
D. deltoides 96, 145
D. 'Doris' 141
D. gratianopolitanus 70, 116
D. 'Gravetye Gem' 81
D. 'Mrs Sinkins' 172
D. 'Pike's Pink' 32, 103
Diascia vigilis 141
Dicentra 'Bacchanal' 104
D. cucullaria 101
D. 'Langtrees' 68
D. 'Stuart Boothman' 68
D. spectabilis 162
D. s. 'Alba' 162
Dictamnus albus purpureus 33
Dierama pulcherrimum 167
Digitalis 112, 219
D. lutea 112
D. × *mertonensis* 112
Dodecatheon meadia 101
Dogwood, see *Cornus*
Doronicum cordatum 21
Dracunculus vulgaris 33
Drumstick primula, see *P. denticulata*
Dryas octopetala 46
Dryopteris borreri cristata 53
D. filix-mas 214

Eccremocarpus scaber 148
Echinops ritro 33
Echium 156
Elaeagnus angustifolia 72, 79
E. × *ebbingei* 'Gilt Edge' 64
E. pungens 'Dicksonii' 64
Elder, see *Sambucus*
Elm 209
Embothrium coccineum 36
E. c. 'Norquinco' 36
Enkianthus campanulatus 39, 125
Epilobium angustifolium album 208
Epimedium 111, 165, 219
E. grandiflorum 'Rose Queen' 104
E. perralderianum 104
E. perralchicum 112
E. × *youngianum* 'Niveum' 104
Eranthis hyemalis 135
Eremurus bungei 167
Erica 107
E. carnea 107
E. × *darleyensis* 107, 139
E. vagans 'Lyonesse' 37
Erodium guttatum 101
E. 'Merstham Pink' 102
Eryngium agavifolium 54
E. bourgatii 35
E. giganteum 54
Erysimum 'Bowles' Mauve' 27
Erythronium 43, 129
E. 'Kondo' 129
E. 'Pagoda' 129
E. 'White Beauty' 129
Escallonia 'Apple Blossom' 204
E. 'Iveyi' 179, 205
Eschscholzia 156
Eucalyptus 18, 85
E. gunnii 88
E. pauciflora subsp. *niphophila* 242
Eucomis bicolor 152
Eucryphia × *nymansensis* 240
Euonymus alatus 125
E. fortunei 'Emerald and Gold' 65
E. f. 'Silver Queen' 17
Eupatorium purpureum 21
Euphorbia characias subsp. *wulfenii* 55
E. cyparissias 112, 219
E. griffithii 'Fireglow' 162
E. mellifera 75
E. myrsinites 33, 103
E. polychroma 35, 60

E. robbiae 215
Euryops acraeus 102

Fagus sylvatica 200, 210
F. s. 'Atropurpurea' 206
Fargesia nitida 220
× *Fatshedera lizei* 46
Fatsia japonica 46, 58
Felicia amelloides 171
Fennel 189, see also *Foeniculum*
Ferns 53, 110, 174
Festuca glauca 114
F. ovina 69
Filipendula rubra 21, 187
Firethorn, see *Pyracantha*
Foeniculum vulgare 114, 189
Forsythia × *intermedia* 120
F. × *i.* 'Lynwood' 120
Fothergilla major 39, 125
Foxglove 112, and see *Digitalis*
Fraxinus 18
Fremontodendron 'California Glory' 149, 179, 222
Fritillaria imperialis 130
F. meleagris 'Aphrodite' 129
Fritillary, see *Fritillaria*
Fuchsia 124, 144
F. 'Coachman' 152
F. 'Dollar Princess' 152
F. 'Lena' 144
F. magellanica 205
F. 'Margaret' 124
F. 'Pink Galore' 153
F. 'Riccartonii' 201
F. 'Thalia' 152

Galanthus nivalis 135
Galega orientalis 34
Galium odoratum 215
Galtonia candicans 132
Garrya elliptica 'James Roof' 205
Gaultheria, see *Pernettya*
Genista aetnensis 240
Gentiana asclepiadea 110, 187
G. a. 'Alba' 110
G. sino-ornata 40, 103
Gentian, see *Gentiana*
Geranium 35, 102, 173, and see also *Pelargonium*
G. cinereum 'Ballerina' 173
G. c. var. *subcaulescens* 'Splendens' 102
G. clarkei 'Kashmir White' 174
G. endressii 105
G. himalayense 'Gravetye' 21
G. 'Johnson's Blue' 105, 162
G. macrorrhizum 105
G. m. 'Bevan's Variety' 174
G. pratense 215
G. psilostemon 162
G. × *riversleaianum* 'Russell Prichard' 170
G. sanguineum var. *striatum* 141
Gingko biloba 247
Gladiolus × *colvillei* 133
Gladwin iris, see *Iris foetidissima*
Gleditsia triacanthos 'Sunburst' 67
Globe artichoke, see *Cynara scolymus*
Glory of the snow, see *Chionodoxa*
Godetia 156
Golden balm 191
Golden hop 62
Gold-leafed Japanese maple, see *Acer shirasawanum* f. *aureum*
Golden rain tree, see *Koelreuteria*
Golden rod, see *Solidago*
Grannies' bonnets, see *Aquilegia vulgaris*
Grape hyacinth, see *Muscari*
Green cotton lavender, see *Santolina rosmarinifolia* subsp. *rosmarinifolia*
Griselinia littoralis 204
Guelder rose, see *Viburnum opulus*
Gunnera manicata 183
Gypsophila 114
G. 'Rosy Veil' 34

Halesia carolina 39
H. monticola 39, 241
Hakonechloa macra 'Alboaurea' 173
× *Halimiocistus wintonensis* 'Merrist Wood Cream' 27
Hamamelis × *intermedia* 'Pallida' 139
H. × *i.* 'Jelena' 37
H. mollis 39
Hart's tongue fern 174, and see *Asplenium scolopendrium*
Hawthorn, see *Crataegus* × *monogyna*
Heather, see *Erica*
Hebe 51, 107, 124
H. albicans 70
H. 'Alicia Amherst' 51
H. 'Boughton Dome' 102
H. × *franciscana* 'Blue Gem' 205
H. 'Great Orme' 51
H. hulkeana 51
H. 'La Séduisante' 51
H. 'Margery Fish' 51
H. 'Mrs Winder' 51
H. 'Pewter Dome' 176
H. pinguifolia 'Pagei' 70, 216
H. 'Purple Queen' 51
H. rakaiensis 107
H. 'Simon Delaux' 51
H. speciosa 51
Hedera 18, 62, 223, 232
H. colchica 'Sulphur Heart' 223
H. helix 'Angularis Aurea' 231
H. h. 'Buttercup' 62
H. h. 'Goldheart' 62
Helenium 35
H. 'Bruno' 168
H. 'Moorheim Beauty' 168
Helianthemum 'Annabel' 96
H.'Wisley Primrose' 114
Helichrysum angustifolium (syn. *italicum*) 70, 85
H. petiolare 153
Helictotrichon sempervirens 70, 86
Heliotropium peruvianum 82, 152
Hellebore 105, 219, and see *Helleborus*
Helleborus argutifolius 53
H. foetidus 113, 175
H. orientalis 137, 165, 175
Hemerocallis 173
H. lilio-asphodelus 82
H. 'Pink Damask' 163
H. 'Summer Wine' 22
Hesperis matronalis 82
Heuchera 111, 175
H. 'Palace Purple' 91
H. 'Rachel' 175
Hibiscus syriacus 'Blue Bird' 28
Himalayan cowslip, see *Primula florindae*
Himalayan poppy, see *Meconopsis*
Hippophae rhamnoides 73
Hoheria lyallii 179
Holly 198, and see *Ilex*
Honesty 216, and see *Lunaria*
Honeysuckle 62, and see *Lonicera*
Hop, see *Humulus*
Hornbeam 209, and see *Carpinus betulus*
Hosta 105, 111, 165 187
H. 'Frances Williams' 175
H. 'Golden Standard' 61
H. 'Halcyon' 69
H. sieboldiana 53, 70
H. s. 'Elegans' 53
H. undulata var. *undulata* 22
Humulus lupulus 'Aureus' 62, 232
Hupeh crab, see *Malus hupehensis*

Hyacinth, see *Hyacinthus*
Hyacinthus orientalis 82
Hydrangeas in variety 146
Hydrangea anomela petiolaris 231
H. arborescens 'Grandiflora' 149, 201
H. 'Blue Wave' 124
H. macrophylla 205
H. m. 'Hamburg' 146
H. paniculata 124
H. 'Preziosa' 146, 177
H. quercifolia 124
H. serrata 'Grayswood' 146
H. villosa 29, 124
Hypericum calycinum 108
H. olympicum 102
Hyssop 189, and see *Hyssopus*
Hyssopus officinalis 85, 189

Iberis 34
I. × *sempervirens* 47, 219
I. umbellatum 34, 157
Ilex 210
I. × *altaclarensis* 'Camelliifolia' 198
I. aquifolium 'Ferox Argentea' 198
I. a. 'Golden Queen' 65
Impatiens 145, 155
Indigofera heterantha 28
Ipomoea 149, 150, 228
Iris 35
Dutch iris 115
Japanese iris, see *I. ensata*
Iris ensata 183
I. foetidissima 113, 219
I. germanica 82, 114
I. innominata 40
I. pseudacorus 'Bastardii' 183
I. reticulata 'Harmony' 136
I. sibirica 'Snow Bounty' 163
I. unguicularis 135
I. versicolor 'Kermesina' 184
I. xiphium 115
Itea ilicifolia 179
Ivy 46, and see *Hedera*

Jacob's ladder, see *Polemonium*
Japanese anemone, see *Anemone* × *hybrida*
Japanese cherry tree 20, and see *Prunus*
Japonica, see *Chaenomeles*
Jasmine, see *Jasminum*
Jasminum nudiflorum 139
J. officinale 79, 148, 232
Jerusalem sage, see *Phlomis*
Joe Pye weed, see *Eupatorium purpureum*
Judas tree, see *Cercis siliquastrum*
Juniperus chinensis 'Aurea' 66, 246
J. communis 'Hibernica' 246
J. horizontalis 'Wiltonii' 108
J. 'Pfizeriana Aurea' 49, 66
J. 'Pfitzeriana Compacta' 49
J. 'Pfitzeriana Glauca' 49
J. sabina tamariscifolia 108
J. virginiana 'Skyrocket' 70, 246

Kaffir lily, see *Schizostylis*
Kalmia angustifolia rubra 37
K. latifolia 'Nimuck Red Bud' 37
Kerria 18
Killarney strawberry tree, see *Arbutus*
Kirengeshoma palmata 43, 169
Kniphofia 55, 165
K. 'Little Maid' 55
K. northiae 55
Koelreuteria paniculata 241
Kolkwitzia amabilis 'Pink Cloud' 28

Laburnum 18, 209, 234
L. × *watereri* 'Vossii' 209
Lady's mantle, see *Alchemilla mollis*
Lady's smock, see *Cardamine pratensis*
Lamium 'Beacon Silver' 70
L. galeobdolon 'Florentinum' 113
L. maculatum 216
L. m. 'Wootton Pink' 22
Lathyrus odoratus 82, 150, 228
Laurel 48, and see *Prunus laurocerasus*
Laurus nobilis 85, 210
Lavender 85, and see *Lavandula*
Lavandula angustifolia 'Hidcote' 70, 207
L. a. 'Munstead' 70
L. × *intermedia* 'Grappenhall' 207
L. lanata 70
Lavatera 'Barnsley' 146
Lawson cypress, see *Chamaecyparis*
Lemon balm, see *Melissa officinalis*
Leopard's bane, see *Doronicum*
Leyland cypress, see × *Cupressocyparis*
Leucojum aestivum 'Gravetye Giant' 131
Leucothöe fontanesiana 39
L. f. 'Rainbow' 93
Lewisia cotyledon 41, 103
Ligularia przewalskii 184
Ligustrum ovalifolium 'Aureum' 65, 206
Lilac 181, and see *Syringa*
Lilium candidum 133
L. martagon 133
L. pardalinum 41
L. 'Pink Perfection' 83
L. regale 'Album' 163
L. speciosum rubrum 43
L. 'Stargazer' 133
Lily 133, and see *Lilium*
Lily-of-the-valley 80, and see *Convallaria*
Lime 209
Linaria maroccana 'Fairy Bouquet' 34
L. purpurea 'Canon Went' 35
Linum 114
L. grandiflorum rubrum 157
L. narbonense 35
L. n. 'Heavenly Blue' 145
Liriodendron 29
Liriope muscari 173
Lithodora diffusa 39
L. d. 'Heavenly Blue' 109
Livingstone daisy, see *Mesembryanthemum*
Lobelia 'Dark Crusader' 170
Lobster claw plant, see *Clianthus*
London pride, see *Saxifraga* × *urbium*
Lonicera fragrantissima 75
L. japonica 'Aureo-reticulata' 62
L. j. 'Halliana' 223
L. nitida 207
L. n. 'Baggesen's Gold' 48, 66
L. periclymenum 'Belgica' 79
L. p. 'Serotina' 79
L. pileata 47
Lords and ladies, see *Arum*
Lotus berthelotii 153
Lovage 190
Love-in-a-mist, see *Nigella*
Love-lies-bleeding, see *Amaranthus*
Lunaria annua 'Alba Variegata' 216
Lungwort, see *Pulmonaria*
Lupin, see *Lupinus*
Lupinus 169
Lychnis chalcedonica 164
L. coronaria alba 35
L. c. atro-sanguinea 35
Lysichiton americanus 184
L. camtschatcensis 185
Lysimachia clethroides 23
L. punctata 23, 187

Madonna lily, see *Lilium candidum*
Magnolia grandiflora 'Exmouth' 75
M. liliiflora 'Nigra' 121
M. × *loebneri* 'Leonard Messel' 237
M. salicifolia 39, 79, 237
M. × *soulangeana* 18, 39, 121
M. × *s.* 'Alba' 237
M. × *s.* 'Brozzoni' 237
M. × *s.* 'Lennei' 237
M. × *s.* 'Rustica Rubra' 237
M. stellata 121
M. wilsonii 76
Mahonia aquifolium 17
M. japonica 58, 79
M. lomariifolia 58
Maidenhair spleenwort, see *Asplenium trichomanes*
Male fern, see *Dryopteris*
Mallow, see *Lavatera*
Maltese cross, see *Lychnis chalcedonica*
Malus 18
M. 'Evereste' 127, 244
M. floribunda 238
M. hupehensis 18
M. × *moerlandsii* 'Profusion' 91, 238
Marigold 190
Marjoram 190
Marsh marigold, see *Caltha*
Matthiola 83
M. fructiculosa alba 76
Meadow cranesbill, see *Geranium pratense*
Meadowsweet 21, and see *Filipendula*
Meconopsis betonicifolia 169
M. cambrica 35, 217
M. × *sheldonii* 43
Melissa officinalis 'Aurea' 61, 85
Mentha gentilis 'Variegata' 191
M. rotundifolia 'Variegata' 84
M. suaveolens 'Variegata' 191
Mertensia virginica 164
Mesembryanthemum 116
Mexican orange blossom, see *Choisya ternata*
Michaelmas daisy 20, and see *Aster*
Milium effusum 'Aureum' 61, 111, 113
Mimulus 'Orange Glow' 185
Mint, see *Mentha*
Miscanthus sinensis 'Silver Feather' 87
Mock Orange 181, and see *Philadelphus*
Moltkia suffruticosa 103
Monarda 85
M. 'Croftway Pink' 169
Morning glory, see *Ipomoea*
Monkshood, see *Aconitum*
Moroccan broom, see *Cytisus battandieri*
Morus nigra 28
Mossy saxifrage 47, 219
'Gaiety' 47
'Pearly King' 47
'Triumph' 47
Mount Etna broom, see *Genista aetnensis*
Mountain avens, see *Dryas octopetala*
Mountain pine, see *Pinus mugo*
Moutan peony, see *Paeonia suffruticosa*
Mulberry tree, see *Morus*
Muscari neglectum 35
Myrrhis odorata 217

Narcissus bulbocodium 136
N. b. romieuxii 136
N. cyclamineus 137
N. 'Golden Harvest' 212
N. 'Ice Follies' 212
N. 'Mount Hood' 131
N. poeticus 'Actaea' 82
N. 'Paper White' 83
N. 'Sir Winston Churchill' 83
N. 'Thalia' 131
Nasturtium 117, 157, 191, and see *Tropaeolum majus*
Nemesia fruticans 155
Nepeta × *faassenii* 69, 165, 173
Nerine bowdenii 134, 219
N. b. 'Fenwick's Variety' 134
New Zealand cabbage palm, see *Cordyline australis*
New Zealand flax, see *Phormium tenax*
Nicotiana 82, 145, 155
Nigella 157
N. 'Miss Jekyll' 157
Nyssa sylvatica 38

Oak, see *Quercus*
Oak-leafed hydrangea, see *Hydrangea quercifolia*
Olearia macrodonta 198, 205
Oleaster, see *Elaeagnus angustifolia*
Omphalodes cappadocica 110
Onion, ornamental, see *Allium*
Onopordum 114
O. acanthium 70
O. arabicum 57, 70
Oregon grape, see *Mahonia aquifolium*
Origanum laevigatum 'Hopley's Variety' 35
O. vulgare 'Aureum' 61, 85
Ornithogalum umbellatum 213
Osmanthus delavayi 79
Osmunda regalis 185
Osteospermum 155
O. ecklonis 142
O. jucundum 217
Othonna cheirifolia 70, 99, 114
Ozothamnus ledifolius 51

Pachysandra 25
Paeonia delavayi 29, 122
P. d. var. *ludlowii* 122, 181
P. lactiflora 'Bowl of Beauty' 164
P. mlokosewitschii 69
P. suffruticosa 'Sitifukujin' 122
Pansy 191
Papaver orientale 'Charming' 169
P. somniferum 157
Paperbark maple, see *Acer griseum*
Parahebe catarractae 97
Parsley 191
Parthenocissus henryana 231
Pasque flower, see *Pulsatilla*
Passiflora caerulea 'Constance Elliot' 229
Passion flower, see *Passiflora*
Peach-leafed bellflower, see *Campanula persicifolia*
Pear, see *Pyrus*
Pelargonium 'Mabel Gray' 85
P. 'Madame Layal' 152
P. 'Purple Unique' 85
P 'Roller's Pioneer' 153
P. tomentosum 85
Pennisetum villosum 35
Penstemon 'Cherry Ripe' 145
P. 'Firebird' 145
P. 'Garnet' 145
P. glaber 176
Pentaglottis sempervirens 218
Peony, see *Paeonia*
Peony flowered poppy, see *Papaver somniferum*
Periwinkle, see *Vinca*
Pernettya 39
P. mucronata 109, 127
Perovskia atriplicifolia 73
Persicaria bistorta 'Superba' 105, 187
P. campanulata 219
Petasites japonicus 23

Petunia 155
Pheasant's eye, see *Narcissus poeticus*
Philadelphus 18
P. 'Belle Etoile' 181
P. 'Manteau d'Ermine' 176
P. 'Sybille' 76
Phlomis fruticosa 114
Phlox adsurgens 'Wagon Wheel' 41, 103
P. paniculata 82
P. p. 'Little Lovely' 169
P. stolonifera 'Ariane' 42
P. subulata 'Emerald Cushion' 97, 103
Phormium tenax 59
Phuopsis stylosa 219
Physalis alkekengi 23
Picea abies 'Gregoryana' 103
P. breweriana 18, 247
P. pungens glauca 'Procumbens' 176
Pieris floribunda 'Forest Flame' 38
P. japonica 'Mountain Fire' 39
Pine, see *Pinus*
Pineapple plant, see *Eucomis*
Pinks 32, and see *Dianthus*
Pinus mugo 49
P. nigra 221
P. radiata 39, 221, 247
P. wallichiana 247
Plane tree, see *Platanus*
Platanus 18
Pleione formosana 42
Polyanthus 142
Polemonium caeruleum 23
P. reptans 'Lambrook Mauve' 164
Polygonatum 25
P. × hybridum 113, 219
Polystichum setiferum 'Divisilobum' 174
P. s. 'Plumosodivisilobum' 89
Poncirus trifoliata 76
Poplar, see *Populus*
Poppy, see *Papaver*
Populus 18
P. alba 221
P. tremula 221
P. 'Robusta' 221
Potentilla fruticosa 'Abbotswood' 146
P. f. 'Elizabeth' 146
P. f. 'Red Ace' 146
P. f. 'Tangerine' 146
Pride of India, see *Koelreuteria*
Primrose 111, and see *Primula vulgaris*
Primula 219
P. auricula 142
P. denticulata 186
P. florindae 186
P. 'Guinevere' 143
P. japonica 111
P. pulverulenta 111, 186
P. 'Valley Red' 186
P. vialii 186
P. vulgaris 111
Privet, see *Ligustrum*
Prunus 18
P. 'Amanogawa' 239
P. × blireana 239
P. cerasifera 'Pissardii' 200, 239
P. 'Kanzan' 19
P. laurocerasus 18, 48, 198
P. l. 'Otto Luyken' 48
P. lusitanica 210
P. pendula 'Pendula Rosea' 243
P. 'Pink Shell' 239
P. serrula 243
P. × subhirtella 'Autumnalis' 241
P. × s. 'Autumnalis Rosea' 241
P. tenella 'Firehill' 29
Pseudosasa japonica 220
Pulmonaria 25, 111, 137, 219
P. rubra 137
P. 'Sissinghurst White' 137
Pulsatilla vulgaris 35
Pyracantha 18, 127, 198, 210, 234
Pyrus 18
P. salicifolia 'Pendula' 73

Quercus 18
Q. cerris 221

Red-hot poker, see *Kniphofia*
Rheum palmatum 'Astrosanguineum' 187
Rhododendron 26, 39, 51
R. Azalea 'Hino-mayo' 177
R. 'Bric-a-Brac' 139
R. 'Elizabeth' 51
R. 'Golden Torch' 121
R. 'Lem's Cameo' 39
R. luteum 39, 77
R. moupinense 139
R. ponticum 220
R. 'Praecox' 121
R. williamsianum 177
Rhodohypoxis baurii 42, 103
Rhus typhina 'Laciniata' 125
Ribes 18
Ricinus communis 'Gibsonii' 152
R. c. 'Impala' 152
Robinia pseudoacacia 'Frisia' 67
Rock rose, see *Helianthemum*
Rodgersia 187
R. pinnata 'Superba' 105
Romneya coulteri 70, 147
Rosa 'Albertine' 232
R. 'Amber Queen' 123, 147
R. 'Bleu Magenta' 233
R. 'Blush Noisette' 233
R. 'Celestial' 73
R. 'Charles de Mills' 78
R. 'Climbing Iceberg' 153
R. 'Constance Spry' 78
R. 'Cornelia' 123
R. 'Escapade' 147
R. filipes 'Kiftsgate' 235
R. 'Fragrant Cloud' 78
R. 'Frau Dagmar Hastrup' 123
R. gallica versicolor, see *R. mundi*
R. glauca 70, 91
R. 'Golden Showers' 149, 232
R. 'Golden Wings' 123
R. 'Guinée' 227
R. 'Iceberg' 149
R. 'Lady Waterlow' 227
R. 'Madame Alfred Carrière' 227
R. 'Madame Gregoire Staechelin' 227
R. 'Mermaid' 149, 227
R. moyesii 'Geranium' 127
R. mundi 203
R. 'Natalie Nypels' 147
R. 'New Dawn' 227, 232
R. 'Paul's Himalayan Musk' 234, 235
R. 'Penelope' 79, 202
R. 'Queen Elizabeth' 202
R. 'Roseraie de l'Hay' 202
R. rubrifolia, see *R. glauca*
R. 'Sweet Juliet' 147
Rose, see *Rosa*
Rose of Sharon, see *Hypericum calycinum*
Rosebay willow herb, see *Epilobium*
Rosemary 191, and see *Rosmarinus*
Rosmarinus officinalis 115, 207
R. o. 'Fastigiatus' 115
R. o. 'Miss Jessopp's Upright' 115
R. o. 'Severn Sea' 115
Rowan, see *Sorbus*
Royal fern, see *Osmunda*
Rubus 18
R. tricolor 17
Rudbeckia 25
R. fulgida 'Goldsturm' 165

Rue, see *Ruta*
Ruta graveolens 85
R. g. 'Jackman's Blue' 71

Sage 85, 115, 191, and see *Salvia*
Sagina subulata 'Aurea' 95
Salix 18
S. elaeagnos 17
S. hastata 'Wehrhahnii' 18
S. helvetica 71
Salvia buchananii 171
S. lavandulifolia 176
S. nemorosa 35
S. n. 'East Friesland' 165
S. officinalis 85, 115,
S. o. 'Icterina' 115
S. o. 'Purpurascens' 115
S. o. 'Tricolor' 115
S. patens 171
S. × *superba* 145, 165
S. × *sylvestris* 'May Night' 165
Sambucus 'Notcutt's Variety' 89
S. racemosa 'Plumosa Aurea' 66
Santolina chamaecyparissus 71, 207
S. pinnata ssp. *neapolitana* 29
S. rosmarinifolia ssp. *rosmarinifolia* 176
Saponaria 25
S. ocymoides 97
Sarcococca hookeriana var. *digyna* 109
Satureja montana 85
Saxifraga × *urbium* 175, 219
Saxifrage 47, 175, and see *Saxifraga* and Mossy saxifrage
Scabiosa caucasica 35
Scabious, see *Scabiosa*
Schizophragma integrifolium 231
Schizostylis coccinea 134
S. 'Sunrise' 134
Sciadopitys verticillata 38
Scilla mischtschenkoana (syn. *tubergeniana*) 137
Sea holly, see *Eryngium*
Sedge, see *Carex*
Sedum album tenuifolium murale 117
S. 'Autumn Joy' 165
S. maximum atropurpureum 91
S. spurium 'Dragon's Blood' 95
S. spathulifolium 'Cape Blanco' 103
Sempervivum 70, 103, 117, 175
S. arachnoideum 'Laggeri' 95
S. 'Commander Hay' 117
Senecio leucostachys 115
S. 'Sunshine', see *Brachyglottis*
Sheep laurel, see *Kalmia angustifolia*
Shooting star, see *Dodecatheon meadia*
Sidalcea 35, 165
Sinacalia tangutica 187
Sinarundinaria, see *Fargesia*
Sisyrinchium striatum 114, 165
Skimmia 18
S. japonica 127, 177
S. j. 'Foremanii' 127
S. j. 'Fragrans' 127
Skunk cabbage, see *Lysichiton*
Smilacina racemosa 43, 82, 111
Smoke bush, see *Cotinus coggygria*
Snapdragon, see *Antirrhinum*
Snowball bush, see *Viburnum opulus* 'Sterile'
Snowdrop 135, and see *Galanthus nivalis*
Snowflake, see *Leucojum*
Solanum crispum 'Glasnevin' 179, 229, 232
Solidago 24
Solomon's seal, see *Polygonatum*
Sorbus 18
S. aria 'Lutescens' 73
S. commixta 245
S. hupehensis 245
S. sargentiana 245
S. vilmorinii 245
Spartina pectinata 'Aureomarginata' 87
Spiderwort, see *Tradescantia*
Spiraea 18
S. 'Arguta' 121
Spurge, see *Euphorbia*
St. Bernard's lily, see *Anthericum liliago*
Stachys macrantha 'Robusta' 24
S. byzantina 69
S. b. 'Silver Carpet' 69
Star of Bethlehem 213, and see *Ornithogalum*
Stinking hellebore, see *Helleborus foetidus*
Stipa gigantea 87, 175
S. tenuissima 87
Stock, see *Matthiola*
Strawberry tree, see *Arbutus*
Sumach, see *Rhus*
Sunrose, see *Cistus*
Sweet cicely, see *Myrrhis*
Sweet pea, see *Lathyrus odoratus*
Sweet rocket, see *Hesperis*
Sweet William 81, and see *Dianthus barbatus*
Symphoricarpus 18
Symphytum caucasicum 25
S. × *uplandicum* 'Variegatum' 93
Syringa 18
S. × *josiflexa* 'Bellicent' 181
S. meyeri 'Palibin' 77
S. 'Missumo' 181

Tamarisk, see *Tamarix*
Tamarix tetrandra 205
Tanacetum densum 'Amani' 70, 99, 103
T. vulgare 219
Tansy, see *Tanacetum vulgare*
Tapestry hedges 199
Taxus 18, 29
T. baccata 49, 199, 210
T. b. 'Aurea' 66
T. b. 'Fastigiata' 246
T. b. 'Semperaurea' 66
T. b. 'Standishii' 66
Telekia speciosa 24, 187
Tellima 25
T. grandiflora 105, 111, 113
T. g. 'Purpurea' 105
Teucrium 29
Thalictrum aquilegiifolium 25
Thrift, see *Armeria*
Thuja occidentalis 199
T. plicata 199
Thunbergia alata 149, 150, 228
Thyme 114, 191, and see *Thymus*
Thymus lanuginosus 70
T. serpyllum 'Coccineus' 95
Tiarella cordifolia 111, 113
Tilia 18
Tobacco flower, see *Nicotiana*
Trachelospermum asiaticum 223
Trachycarpus fortunei 57
Tradescantia 165
T. virginiana 'Purple Dome' 145
T. v. 'Isis' 145
T. v. 'J.C. Weguelin' 145
T. v. 'Osprey' 145
Tree mallow, see *Lavatera*
Tricyrtis formosana 42
Trifolium repens 'Purpurascens' 95
Trillium grandiflorum 43
T. g. roseum 43
Trollius chinensis 'Golden Queen' 187
Tropaeolum majus 117, 145, 150, 157, 228
T. speciosum 39
Tsuga canadensis 'Pendula' 49
Tupelo 38, and see *Nyssa*
Tulip 131, and see *Tulipa*

Tulipa 'Burgundy' 131
T. kaufmanniana 'Gaiety' 131
T. sprengeri 213
T. sylvestris 213
T. tarda 213
Turk's cap lily, see *Lilium martagon*
Turkey oak, see *Quercus cerris*

Umbrella pine, see *Sciadopitys verticillata*
Umbrella plant, see *Darmera*

Valerian, see *Centranthus*
Valeriana phu 'Aurea' 61
Veratrum nigrum 89
V. album 89
Verbascum 114
Verbena 145, 155
V. bonariensis 35
V. 'Sissinghurst' 153
Veronica austriaca ssp. *teucrium* 'Corfu Form' 173
V. incana 70
V. pinnata 'Blue Eyes' 103
V. prostrata (syn. *rupestris*) 35, 97, 219
V. spicata subsp. *incana* 99
Viburnum 18, 234
V. × *bodnantense* 'Dawn' 77
V. davidii 109, 177
V. × *juddii* 79, 121
V. opulus 'Sterile' 203
V. o. 'Xanthocarpum' 127, 203
V. plicatum 'Mariesii' 59
V. rhytidophyllum 59
V. tinus 210, 220
Vinca 18, 111
V. major 111
V. minor 111
V. m. 'Burgundy' 219
Vine, see *Vitis*
Viola 111, 191, 219
V. 'Bowles' Black' 143
V. cornuta 'Alba' 143
V. c. 'Lilacina' 143
V. 'Irish Molly' 143
V. 'Jackanapes' 143
V. labradorica 35, 91, 113
V. odorata 82, 137
Violet 137, and see *Viola*
Vitis 'Brant' 232
V. coignetiae 230, 232, 234, 235
V. vinifera 'Purpurea' 230, 232

Wandflower, see *Dierama*
Wake-robin, see *Trillium grandiflorum*
Wallflower 27, and see *Cheiranthus*
Weigela 18
W. florida 'Foliis Purpureis' 19, 91
W. f. 'Variegata' 93
Welsh poppy, see *Meconopsis cambrica*
Whitebeam, see *Sorbus aria*
White sage, see *Artemisia ludoviciana*
Willow 17, and see *Salix*
Willow gentian, see *Gentiana asclepiadea*
Winter aconite, see *Eranthis*
Winter savory 191, and see *Satureja*
Wintersweet, see *Chimonanthus*
Wisteria floribunda 230, 232
W. f. 'Macrobotrys' 230
W. sinensis 230, 232
W. s. 'Black Dragon' 230
W. s. 'Caroline' 79
Witch hazel, see *Hamamelis*
Wood anemone, see *Anemone nemorosa*
Woodruff, see *Galium*
Woolly willow, see *Salix lanata*

Xanthoceras sorbifolium 29

Yarrow 30, and see *Achillea*
Yew 208, 234, and see *Taxus*
Yucca 70, 114
Y. filamentosa 57
Y. flaccida 57
Y. gloriosa 57
Y. recurvifolia 57

Zantedeschia aethiopeca 'Crowborough' 132, 187

Acknowledgements

Many of the photographs were taken in the author's garden. The publishers would also like to thank the many people and organizations whose gardens have appeared in this book, including the following: Barnsley House, Barnsley, Cirencester; Burford House, Tenbury Wells; Chilcombe House, Chilcombe, Dorset; Dr A. and Dr. L. Cox, Woodpeckers, Marlcliff, Bidford-on-Avon; Denmans, Denmans Lane, Fontwell; Eastgrove Cottage Garden Nursery, Sankyns Green, Shrawley, Worcester; Richard Edwards, Well Cottage, Blakemere; Frampton Manor, Frampton; The Hon Mrs Peter Healing, The Priory, Kemerton; Lance Hattatt, Arrow Cottage, Ledgemoor, Weobley; Hergest Croft, Kington; Hodges Barn, Shipton Moyne; Kim Hurst, The Cottage Herbery, Boraston, Tenbury Wells; Kiftsgate Court, near Chipping Campden; Oxford Botanic Gardens; Mrs Richard Paice, Bourton House Garden, Bourton-on-the-Hill, Moreton-in-Marsh; The Picton Garden, Colwall; Anthony Poulton, 21 Swinton Lane, Worcester; Powis Castle (National Trust); Tony Ridler, 7 St Peters Terrace, Cockett, Swansea; Royal Botanic Gardens, Kew; RHS Garden, Wisley; Paul and Betty Smith, The Old Chapel, Ludlow; Stone House Cottage, Kidderminster; Raymond Treasure, Stockton Bury Gardens, Kimbolton; The Weir, Swainshill, Hereford (National Trust); Wakehurst Place (National Trust); Whitfield, Wormbridge.

The photograph on the front cover shows part of Rosemary Verey's garden at Barnsley House, Gloucestershire, in spring.